To Kerry
Love and
from Barrie...

Barrie Mahoney worked as a teacher and head teacher in the south west of England, and then became a school inspector in England and Wales. A new life and career as a newspaper reporter in Spain's Costa Blanca led to him launching and editing an English language newspaper in the Canary Islands. Barrie's books include novels in 'The Prior's Hill Chronicles' series, as well as books for expats in the 'Letters from the Atlantic' series, which give an amusing and reflective view of life abroad.

Barrie writes regular columns for newspapers and magazines in Spain, Portugal, Ireland, Australia, South Africa, Canada, UK and the USA. He also designs websites to promote the Canary Islands and living and working abroad, and is often asked to contribute to radio programmes about expat life.

Although Barrie believes strongly in being part of the European family, he reluctantly returned to the UK in 2019, and now lives with his partner David, corgi Oscar and Merlin the cat in South Devon. He is a committed Quaker (The Religious Society of Friends), which continues to have a significant influence upon his life.

Visit the author's website:

http://barriemahoney.com

Other books by Barrie Mahoney

Journeys & Jigsaws (The Canary Islander Publishing) 2013
ISBN: 978-0957544475 (Paperback and eBook)

Threads and Threats (The Canary Islander Publishing) 2013
ISBN: 978-0992767105 (Paperback and eBook)

Letters from the Atlantic (The Canary Islander Publishing) 2013
ISBN: 978-0992767136 (Paperback and eBook)

Living the Dream (The Canary Islander Publishing) 2015
ISBN: 978-0992767198 (Paperback and eBook)

Expat Survival (The Canary Islander Publishing) 2015
ISBN: 978-0992767167 (Paperback and eBook)

Message in a Bottle (The Canary Islander Publishing) 2016
ISBN: 978-0995602700 (Paperback and eBook)

Escape to the Sun (The Canary Islander Publishing) 2016
ISBN: 978-0957544444 (Paperback and eBook)

Expat Voice (The Canary Islander Publishing) 2014
ISBN: 978-0992767174 (Paperback and eBook)

Island in the Sun (The Canary Islander Publishing) 2015
ISBN: 978-0992767181 (Paperback and eBook)

Footprints in the Sand (The Canary Islander Publishing) 2016 ISBN: 978-0995602717 (Paperback and eBook)

Living in Spain and the Canary Islands (The Canary Islander Publishing) 2017 ISBN: 978-0995602724 (Paperback and eBook)

Letters from the Canary Islands and Spain (The Canary Islander Publishing) 2018 ISBN: 978-0995602731 (Paperback and eBook)

Secrets and Lies (The Canary Islander Publishing) 2020 ISBN: 978-0995602748 (Paperback and eBook)

Travelling Hopefully

Barrie Mahoney

The Canary Islander Publishing

© Copyright 2022

Barrie Mahoney

The right of Barrie Mahoney to be identified as author of this work has been asserted by him in accordance with the Copyright, Designs and Patents Act 1988.

All Rights Reserved

No reproduction, copy or transmission of this publication may be made without written permission. No paragraph of this publication may be reproduced, copied or transmitted save with the written permission of the author, or in accordance with the provisions of the Copyright Act 1956 (as amended).
Any person who commits any unauthorised act in relation to this publication may be liable to criminal prosecution and civil claims for damages.
A CIP catalogue record for this title is available from the British Library.

ISBN 978-0995602755
www.barriemahoney.com

First Published in 2022

The Canary Islander Publishing

Acknowledgements

I would like to thank all those people that I have met on my journey to where I am now and to my partner, David, for his love and support, as well as for his proof-reading skills.

To supportive friends who helped me to overcome the many problems and frustrations that I faced, and taught me much about learning to adapt to a new culture. Also, to friends in the UK and those scattered around the world, who kept in touch despite being so far away.

With grateful thanks to our good friend, Shiou Tsai, for his design expertise in creating this book cover.

Disclaimer

This book is about real people, real places and real events, but the names of people and companies have been changed to avoid any embarrassment.

Dedication

This book is dedicated to the 'New Europeans'; those who have decided to leave the country of their birth and to start a new life in Europe, and for those working to restore the UK's place within the European family.

Contents

Preface	14
Setting the Scene	18
All Change	30
Flying Cats and Dogs	42
Not Good, Not Bad, Just Different	57
Taking Back Control … With Flags	65
Expats and Immigrants	76
Police and Crime	84
Orchids, Gardening and Cats	93
This Won't Hurt a Bit	104
When It's Gone, It's Gone	112
A Nice Cup of Coffee	119
Empty Shelves and Empty Pumps	125
The Parish Sweeper	132
Superfast Internet Connection	140
The National Health Service	148
It's Not a Proper Barbeque Unless It's Burnt	159
Charity Shops	167
A Nice Cup of Tea	173
The Veggie Option	180
Motoring in Spain	187
Bills, Bills and More Bills	194
Pets and Vets	204
Something is rotten in the state of Denmark	213
The Banking Business	223
World Beating or What?	231
A Spiritual Journey	238
The Elephant in the Room	249
It Ain't Over Until the Fat Lady Sings	253

Preface

When we returned to the UK to live in 2019, I thought that my tenth book about living and working abroad 'Letters from the Canary Islands and Spain' would be the last 'Letters from the Atlantic' that I would publish. After all, what would be the point of writing about living on a sunny island in the Atlantic, when we had moved to cloudy, damp Devon? I had another novel to write, which would keep me busy, and I would finally say goodbye to writing about living and working in another country.

It was an email from an editor of one of the magazines that I write for that changed my mind, and is responsible for this book. He asked why I had not recently sent him any submissions for his magazine? When I reminded him that I had moved back to the UK and could see little point in further articles, he responded by saying, "Why not? Many Brits are returning, or attempting to return, to the UK because of Brexit. Share your experiences of the issues that you are facing. I'm convinced that your experiences will be a help to many people, as well as entertaining for the rest of us."

It is with these words that the idea of 'Travelling Hopefully' was born. In many ways, this book is a sequel to my first book 'Letters from the Atlantic' which tells of our early life in Spain and the Canary Islands.

This book reflects upon the experiences that David and I encountered on our return to the UK, during a time of Brexit uncertainties, rapidly followed by lengthy Covid lockdowns, amidst a rapidly changing political and social landscape with a potential war in Europe on the horizon.

I compare incidents and our life in the Canary Islands to our new life in Devon, which may be annoying to some, since it is also a commentary on the political and social changes that I see around me; it is a subjective view, of course. Over the sixteen years or so that we have been out of the UK, there have been many changes, with very few for the better, it seems.

Life in Gran Canaria was not as perfect as many may imagine, but looking back, life in the UK now seems more complicated, divided, jingoistic, harsher, and with indifferent concern for other people.

It is also a country in political and social crisis, which those who live here seem unable or unwilling to recognise. There is a paucity of political leadership from any political party, and populism has taken an unhealthy grip on the nation, no doubt following in the steps of the US.

I am shocked at the increase in levels of poverty, the growing number of foodbanks, the rise in racism, knife and gang violence, as well as a growing and deliberately fostered hostility towards Europe, fanned by a powerful group of right-wing politicians and wealthy fanatics, be they known as oligarchs or simply as 'Tory Grandees'.

I was once asked, "So, why didn't you stay where you were, if you like Europe so much?" The truth is that often I wish that we had. However, we were already well aware of souring relationships between the EU and the UK, issues with both healthcare and getting older, as well as missing family and friends.

More will be discussed about this later in the book. Has it worked out as well as we had hoped? In some ways, no. Our plans to meet up with family and friends have, so far, been put on hold due to Covid. We miss the island, the healthy climate, the outdoor lifestyle, and the non-judgemental attitudes of those who live and work there.

In many ways, I feel that I have aged twenty years in the short time that we have been back in the UK, and I gather that this is not an unusual comment from those returning from a life in the sun. Above all, we miss our Spanish and European friends. On the plus side, when Covid issues settle, we will once again be able to visit family and friends again.

We will be able to revisit some of our favourite places, and enjoy the beautiful Devon countryside. We will be able to visit garden centres and enjoy cream teas, as well as speaking our native language, which I have missed.

Since I began writing this book, I have been diagnosed with bowel and liver cancer. So far, the diagnosis, tests and surgery have been excellent, and I am grateful to have returned to the UK in time to deal with this life changing chapter of my life.

I know that treatment in Spain would have been at least as good as the care that I am currently receiving, but it is reassuring to have returned to the UK where I can rely upon close family and friends for support, and not have to worry about the language when dealing with complicated medical and treatment issues.

The tragic passing of a dear friend in Gran Canaria has made me realise that I am fortunate to be back in the UK, given my current circumstances, since end-of-life care and hospice support are sadly lacking in the Canary Islands and much of Spain.

In a tongue in cheek comment, I made the point that this book should not be read by Brexiteers or those who are fans of Boris Johnson, since it is most likely to offend, or at least annoy. I don't regret this remark, since I believe that both are two of the main factors that are responsible for the current attitudes in the UK. The UK is currently in a state of flux, but the reasons for its malaise stem much deeper than Johnson and Brexit.

Anti-European, and indeed anti-foreigner attitudes, have been developed and cultivated in the UK for the last forty years or so, and have culminated in a whole range of divisive issues that cross over the usual political divides. Brexit, Johnson and Truss, as well as the supporting cabal of Europe haters, are merely the unpleasant discharge from a lingering poisonous boil that will eventually be lanced, treated and forgotten. Maybe, over time, Brexiteers will be proved right, but I doubt it.

Setting the Scene

The Ukrainians voted for a comedian and got a leader. A man with an unerring moral compass. We in the UK also voted for a comedian and got exactly that.

Monday 4 August 2003 is a date that we will always remember. This was the day when we left the UK and began our new lives in Spain. Our home in Bournemouth was for sale, and we had bought a small villa in the Costa Blanca.

Our Bournemouth home had already been emptied by Pickford's Removals, and we hoped our house contents were already on their way to our new home in Rojales, which is near to Alicante in Spain's Costa Blanca. It was an exciting, and exhausting time, but we were both full of hope and expectations for our new life in the sun.

We had travelled to Southampton on the previous evening and checked in at an airport hotel. It was there that we had dinner and said farewell to good friends who had taken the trouble to see us off. It was a strange feeling, knowing that we would not live in the country again for some considerable time, if ever.

We had made a serious commitment to Spain; a country that we had visited many times in the past and loved. It was time for us to make a choice and live in the country of our choosing and not based upon an accident of birth.

It was a very hot day and we sat on the airport runway in a Flybe plane waiting for take-off. There had already been a delay, but the luggage had been loaded and there were several people being busy around the plane. Finally, the captain made an announcement on the speaker system. As it was such a hot day our plane would not be able to take off from the short Southampton runway with the number of people and luggage on board, otherwise there would not be enough fuel to get us to Alicante.

We had a choice, we could either leave our luggage behind, which would follow us on a later flight, and fly direct to Alicante, or they could fly passengers and luggage to Bournemouth Airport, which has a longer runway, refuel, and then take off for Alicante. The very thought of flying to Spain without any luggage was a horrific idea; there was a show of hands, and most passengers voted to fly to Bournemouth and onwards with luggage intact.

The irony of returning to Bournemouth for the beginning of our journey when we had taken the trouble to travel to Southampton and stay a night in the airport hotel was not missed upon us. Still, the flight around Bournemouth on a cloudless day when we finally took off made up for the previous disappointment in Southampton.

It was a kind of farewell tour of a town that we knew so well and loved. It had been our home together for many years and a town that I had known well since childhood when we used to visit Aunt Gertie for our annual holiday.

For those unfamiliar with my early writing, I will explain briefly here why we made the decision to move to Spain. David, my partner, had been very ill following a breakdown in his health.

As a committed headteacher with an onerous teaching commitment, David's school had become 'Grant Maintained'. This was a devious strategy devised by the Thatcher Government to wrestle control of schools away from local education authorities, by supposedly giving them greater autonomy, as well as significantly increased budgets, since funds would no longer be diverted to the local education authority.

For small schools struggling with budgets and potential losses of staff, it seemed to be a solution to several problems and was jumped upon by many governing bodies who were attracted by the cash deal without giving it detailed examination of the downsides. The proposal was promoted by school governors and then voted upon by parents.

Sadly, David's school voted to become Grant Maintained, whilst the parents at my own school thankfully saw sense, and voted overwhelmingly against it.

Although the shift in status meant that David's school received additional funding and could retain an additional teacher, it meant considerable administrative work for the school.

In larger schools the additional burdens fell upon newly appointed administrative staff, as well as willing and able professionally-minded school governors. In David's case, the new burdens fell upon David and his secretary, with little responsibility being accepted by school governors.

As David was already under pressure from his teaching commitments, he could no longer cope and became very ill. He was told he could no longer work and placed on medication for life.

At the same time, I was working as a school inspector for OFSTED in England and Estyn in Wales, as well as advisory work for several schools. A new Chief Inspector had been appointed, later accompanied by yet another modified version of 'the framework' upon which we were to base our judgements of the performance of schools that we were inspecting.

We were asked to attend a meeting in Plymouth, and it was during the late morning session that I suddenly realised that the new framework due to be implemented in September had not yet been released to schools. It was already the beginning of July, yet schools due to be inspected in the Autumn term had no knowledge of the revisions that they would be judged against.

I also realised that the criteria were now considerably harsher than currently operating, so that schools that previously performed as 'satisfactory' would now fail with all the serious consequences that would follow.

Although I was primarily a teacher, I thoroughly enjoyed my work as a school inspector, since it placed me in an ideal position to witness some outstanding work, as well as meeting and working with many gifted teachers.

OFSTED is rarely a popular organisation with teachers, parents or the general British public, but I was always felt it to be an essential part of monitoring the performance of our schools, and was pleased to be part of it.

It was a privilege to experience children learning from high quality teaching. Occasionally, the performance of some schools was unsatisfactory, and sometimes poor, yet it was my responsibility to ensure that issues within the school were identified and corrected as a matter of urgency. All children have a right to high quality education, and it was the responsibility of OFSTED and others, such as myself, to ensure that this was done.

The Plymouth meeting unsettled me, and I left the meeting with a feeling of unfairness and underhandedness in the way that inspections would proceed in the Autumn term.

It was at that point I decided to leave the work that I had enjoyed for the last seven years and, in view of David's health, to begin the new life in the sun, which we had often discussed.

We immediately felt at home in the Costa Blanca. We had friendly supportive neighbours, some of whom became, and still are, good friends. David made a rapid recovery to his old self, and within weeks had ceased to take any medication.

After a few months, David had been appointed as manager of an office for an English language newspaper in Torrevieja, and I quickly followed as a reporter for the same newspaper. These were exciting times for both of us and, thanks to the newspaper, helped us to settle and understand more about our adopted country.

Two years later, our boss realised our potential and raised the idea about opening a new newspaper in a different part of Spain. We suggested the Canary Islands as a possibility, and our boss asked us to let him have a business plan.

A few days later we submitted a detailed plan, which was agreed. Two weeks later our lovely new home in the Costa Blanca had been placed for sale with estate agents, and we were on our way to the Canary Islands with our dogs, Barney and Bella, and a laptop computer to launch and manage a new English language newspaper, initially in Gran Canaria.

At that time, it was a three-day sea voyage from Cadiz and quite an adventure. More details of our move to and life in the Costa Blanca are covered in my first book 'Letters from the Atlantic'.

Reflections of life working on the island are also covered in subsequent publications, which I will not repeat here, because I now need to explain some of our reasons for moving back to the UK in 2019. Let us now fast forward…

The next few years saw the debate around Brexit becoming more prominent in the national debate. I was certainly aware that the European Union was, for some people, becoming an unpopular concept in the UK. Looking back, I recall stories such as 'Bendy Bananas', which were heavily ridiculed in newspapers such as the Daily Mail, Daily Express and the Sun.

Apparently, the EU were attempting to ban straight and bendy bananas, and generally meddling in areas that they were not required to meddle. As a journalist working on the islands, amidst many bananas, myself and others quickly realised what nonsense this myth was and wrote articles to the contrary.

This was the first time that I had heard a name that would become familiar over the next few years, and eventually destroy our lives and that of many living in a European Union country.

That name was Boris Johnson, and I clearly remember reading his ridiculous story about 'Bendy Bananas', and writing my own article pointing out the nonsense and inaccuracy of this unfortunate drivel.

This article was to be one of the first of Johnson's many lies, believed and supported by the Telegraph, Daily Mail, Daily Express and the Sun. Other anti-EU stories such as this quickly followed, aided by a right-wing media campaign, and were gobbled up as `true' by a gullible, and often foolish, British public.

It was at that time that I became well aware of what I initially dismissed as a publicity seeking opportunist, namely a reporter called Alexander Boris de Pfeffel Johnson. Johnson, who was reporting from Brussels at the time, was intent upon making a name for himself by distorting facts into what he regarded as amusing and mocking 'reality'.

One such story that I recall was the headline that "Italy fails to measure up on condoms", blaming EU bureaucrats for their refusal to accept requests from Italy for a smaller size. Thirty years later, even Johnson's editor at the Telegraph commented that he was exasperated by the "load of bullshit" written by Johnson.

He went on to say "Johnson was the paramount of exaggeration, distortion and lies. He was a clown - a successful clown." This 'buffoonery' or 'clown like' behaviour is, of course, a form of studied eccentricity, and cleverly designed to appeal to less perceptive members of the British public.

Judging from the behaviour of other Etonians, I suspect this was part of the 'core curriculum' cultivated successfully at prestigious schools, such as Eton.

Whether it is hanging from that well publicised zip wire as Mayor of London, or making one of those familiar, but deliberate 'gaffs' is all part of a well-designed publicity machine to endear Johnson to a less than critical British public.

Although not unique, Johnson sought out niche and potentially controversial pieces of EU regulation and turned them into front page stories about threats to UK sovereignty, which an unthinking British public up lapped up. Johnson is often said to be an "intelligent man" by his supporters, but I have my doubts. It is clear, however, that Johnson has a Thesaurus-type brain that easily remembers complex words and phrases, even in Latin, which he delights in using whenever he wishes to impress or to appear 'statesmanlike'.

Psychologists often refer to this approach as a form of camouflage, designed to hide other weaknesses, such as an inability to communicate and relate meaningfully to others. Whether or not these words form an intelligent sentence and not just a 'meaningless babble of incomprehensible words' is for others to decide.

It is testament to the success of Johnson's public relations machine that most of the British public now refer to him simply as 'Boris' and not 'Johnson', as if they know him personally. Do you recall Theresa May being referred to as 'Theresa', or David Cameron being referred to simply as 'David' in the popular press or by your friends and next-door neighbours? I somehow doubt it.

Although I will not dwell too much on what I see as the failings of the then British Prime Minister, which I will leave to others, I do see his intervention as one of the reasons behind the ongoing disaster that is Brexit.

Johnson's five years working as a Telegraph reporter in Brussels shaped his politics and had a significant influence upon the wider British Eurosceptic movement. He was, of course, joined later by other self-seeking publicists, such as Nigel Farage and those who saw an opportunity to reshape the country in their own image. Sadly, facts were of little importance in the debate about the UK's continuing membership of the European Union, as Johnson and others had discovered.

Although it is fair to say that I regard those who voted for Brexit as misguided, I do respect those who can give an articulate, consistent and well-reasoned arguments for their decision. I have little time for those who were merely influenced by foolish articles and fairy tales that appear in the Mail, Sun and Express, and no time or respect at all for those characters seeking personal popularity and aggrandisement, such as Johnson.

Research clearly shows that Johnson was never a committed Brexiter, but someone who wavered many times between his support for the EU, as well as for leaving.

In 2001, Johnson wrote that "Britain's interests were still on balance served by maintaining our membership, and that withdrawal would mean a worrying loss of influence". In 2003, Johnson told the House of Commons "I am not by any means an ultra-Eurosceptic. In some ways, I am a bit of a fan of the European Union. If we did not have one, we would invent something like it." Later reports also show that this finely balanced argument was only decided by Johnson at the last minute, as a cynical step towards gaining the premiership of the UK.

Looking back to those years, despite the warning signs, I did not at that time regard the increased anti-EU feeling as a serious threat to our continuing membership. Maybe I was in denial of what could happen?

As a reporter on the islands, I had many opportunities to meet with and discuss the issue with British Embassy and consular staff, as well as with those in the know in Brussels, but it was rarely seen as a serious threat to the stability of the UK and British immigrants living in Europe.

It was initially disbelief, followed by a great shock and sadness when we awoke to the news that the UK had voted to leave the European Union.

When David and I left Gran Canaria to live in our new home in South Devon, I ceased writing my weekly articles for several newspapers and magazines. I felt that I had little more to offer; the job was done and that I could only write about my experiences whilst living in Spain and the Canary Islands. It was time to close that chapter in my life and to move on.

More recently, I was surprised to receive an email from an editor of a newspaper that I had worked with for many years asking me why I was no longer submitting articles to him. I explained my reasons to him, pointing out that I could no longer report and comment about Spain from the UK.

He disagreed and told me that readers would like to know why and how we had returned to life in the UK, how we were adjusting, and the differences that we had noticed in the time that we had lived in Spain. He also made the point that there were still many British immigrants living in Europe who felt that they should return to the UK following the Brexit vote, but do not have the means to do so.

I took the editor's advice, and I hope that our experiences will prove to be of interest, as well as giving some explanation and showing empathy with those who are dealing with the dramatic change in culture and attitudes that they will experience in returning from Europe to live in the UK. It is by no means an easy transition, and it is for those who are still living in Europe, as well as those who have returned to the UK, that I dedicate this book.

All Change

Thursday 23 June 2016. This was the day when my life changed, and that of thousands of other British nationals, as we moved into an unpredictable direction. Whether it is a change for the worse or for the better, only time will tell.

Those of us of a certain age are supposed to be able to say without any doubt what we were doing on the day that Princess Diana died. No doubt because I am not a devout Royalist, I have no recollection of that day, but I do remember very clearly what I was doing on the day when the Twin Towers were destroyed, together with the horrific loss of life.

We were having broadband Internet installed at the time and were convinced that the horrors playing out on our computer screen were from a disaster movie that we had stumbled upon.

Another day that will always remain firmly etched in my memory is the day following the referendum to leave the European Union, that of Thursday 23 June 2016.

Referendum Day had been a very happy and memorable day for us. My partner, David, and I were in the UK celebrating the marriage of two very good friends. We had been away from the UK for some time, and it was good to meet up with old friends again and to participate in a celebration of love that this special day was all about.

We didn't think too much about the referendum; we had already voted by post and although the result was uncertain, we and others that we spoke to were reasonably confident that common sense would shine through. The hate, lies and suspicions that had been generated during the referendum campaign would be defeated once and for all.

Later that day, as were on our way to the airport, we became less certain. We were surprised to see so many obviously hastily constructed banners, union flags and gaudy posters promoting the Brexit cause.
As we drove through several towns on our way to the airport, we were met with groups of people waving Brexit banners on roundabouts.

Worryingly, we saw very few EU flags and posters promoting remaining within the EU: it was all very strange, and not what we had been led to believe from the mainstream media. The news that we were picking up on our mobile phones also indicated that the vote would be very close. We boarded our flight home, keeping our finger crossed that the following day would bring us the news that we were desperately hoping for.

We woke up early on Friday 24 June and immediately switched on the television news. The newsreader calmly, yet gravely repeated the news that the UK had decided in favour of leaving the European Union.

We were shocked and sat in silence for some time as the impact of the news gradually hit us; we knew that life would never be the same again for ourselves and many others. The ability to choose where we should live and work and not through the accident of birth would be taken away from us.

Later that morning, we met our Spanish friends and acquaintances in our village, and were met with hugs, tears and words of consolation. Our German friends were more to the point, "Will you be staying here?" they asked in their kindly, but usual direct manner. We mumbled something along the lines of it being too early to decide, and that we couldn't see why things should change in such a way that we would need to leave our wonderful island.

No, things would continue very much as they had before. How wrong we were.

As a reporter and regular blogger, I was used to receiving comments, criticism and requests for advice and assistance from readers of my newspaper articles and blogs from readers in Spain, as well as other parts of the world that had a significant British immigrant population.

Following the referendum result, my mailbox became full of comments from British residents bemoaning the referendum result. Many of the emails were troubling, whilst others were heart-breaking.

It was mainly the elderly British residents who had serious health issues and were being well looked after within the Spanish healthcare service that were particularly concerned. Some were anxious to return to the UK, but their small pensions and lack of capital meant that they could not afford to return to the UK.

Many were very concerned that they would no longer be covered by the valuable and reciprocal health scheme that Spain had with the UK, and they could not afford the high costs of private health insurance. Pensions were another area of great concern; would they continue to be linked to the UK cost of living?

Those residents who had been fortunate enough to buy their own homes, including ourselves, were also becoming well aware of the rapid drop in house prices, as well as the falling pound. Some residents who had purchased homes recently with the help of a mortgage from a Spanish bank were likely to face negative equity when they came to sell.

Those on fixed pensions who had benefitted from a strong pound-euro exchange rate in the past, were now aware of the rapid fall in the value of their pensions. There were also suggestions that UK pensioners would cease to benefit from pension increases once the UK had left the EU.

During this initial period of turbulence, the British and Spanish governments, as well as the European Union did their best to curb unnecessary anxiety. British Embassy and Consular officials were overwhelmed with questions about what would happen, but due to the vagueness and lack of planning for a 'Leave' vote, the reassurance of officials sounded hollow and lacked conviction, which was quickly picked up by anxious British residents.

As a reporter, my own discussions with Spanish and British Embassy officials led me also to be concerned, particularly as many of the replies to questions involved the word 'reciprocity', meaning that Spain intended to treat British citizens equally fairly and in a similar manner that the UK treated Spanish and European citizens in the UK.

I heard similar reassuring comments from colleagues and friends working in France, Germany and Italy. Were these reassurances to be believed? Hearing the increasing bullish and angry rhetoric coming from the UK led to a rapid decrease in confidence that anyone would be treated fairly at all. The genie was well and truly out of the bottle and, once out, could never be put back inside.

During the ensuing months, there was much rhetoric from the British Government, as well as the European Union. The initial spirit of cooperation soon changed to hostility, aided and abetted by the right-wing British press, as well as self-seeking politicians who could see opportunities for publicity and eventual promotion.

Green and white papers were published, promises made and assurances given. British Embassy and Consulate staff were kept busy reassuring anxious residents. Many meetings were held by well-meaning consular staff intended to answer many of the questions, often repeated, by residents who demanded to know what would happen if?

Confident answers were usually given, but many of us were aware that no one really knew what would happen, no one had an answer, because the leave scenario had not been thought possible or planned for.

Although I attended the first two of these 'Question and Answer' sessions, I stopped going when I realised that, without sounding too arrogant, many residents, including ourselves, already knew rather more than the consular staff. Indeed, anyone who switched on the radio and read a variety of newspapers quickly realised that, at this stage in the negotiations, there were no answers, so what was the point of speculation?

Despite this, there was some very useful advice from the British Consulate; namely to ensure that all our documents were in order. Spain, as well as other European nations are renowned for their bureaucratic processes; many administrative staff love nothing more than to deny or delay a particular administrative process.

There's nothing vindictive or personal about this, it is just the way that they do things. Even the most trivial omission can lead to lengthy delays or even a hefty fine for the transgression.

Upon checking, we quickly realised that our residency documents needed to be upgraded to the current issue, which we did as soon as possible at the local police station.

One piece of advice that we were grateful to have ignored, or forgotten about, was the requirement for British nationals living in Spain to exchange their UK driving licences for Spanish ones.

During our first months in Spain, we did attempt to do this with a visit to the department responsible for motoring matters, Trafico. The clerk on duty gave our UK licences a cursory glance, and then announced that it was not necessary to exchange them as we were European citizens, so why would we want to do this? We agreed.

After that experience, despite advice to the contrary, we continued to hold on to our UK driving licences. In view of our planned return to the UK, we were pleased that we had held on to them.

Prime Minister Cameron quickly resigned after the referendum. This was followed by a troubling period of government led Prime Minister May, who was full of good intentions in promoting an agreement that would ensure that many of the benefits that the UK had enjoyed through membership of the European Union over the last 40 years would continue.

Whilst history may in time agree that Mrs May was broadly correct in her aims, Brexiteers (as they came to be known) vehemently disagreed with a policy that was seen not to fulfil the aims of the Leave vote.

Again, aided and abetted by the right-wing press, and the support of an angry British public, who could smell the spillage of blood, led to unhappiness and confusion for those of us left on the receiving end of these verbal and often poisonous spats, as we were anxious to continue with our lives within our adopted European countries.

I must admit that at this stage, along with many other British nationals, I held the view that as the referendum was supposed to be purely 'advisory', there would be a second referendum to confirm or reject the original vote. This was not a popular view in the UK, and the ensuing vitriol and scorn poured upon those who supported the idea was unpleasant, but there seemed to be a real possibility that this would happen.

This delusion lasted for only a very short time, and it soon became very clear that the referendum result was here to stay, and we would all just have to put up with the consequences. The Brexit referendum quickly became a source of division and anger between families and friends. Discussion of the subject was usually not a good idea at the dinner table, together with sex, religion and politics.

Some families held such divided views that even to this day the hurt has not been forgiven or forgotten.

I too recall a troubling conversation with two of our very good friends who were visiting the island. One of them cheerfully admitted that they had voted 'Leave'.

We were horrified, but our friends justified their action by adding that they had not fully understood the implications of a 'Leave' vote, but regretted voting in the way that they had, as they could see now that it could really disrupt plans for their many holidays within Europe.

Besides, they had also heard that mobile phone roaming charges would be reintroduced once the UK left the EU, which would lead to horrendously high bills when they were out of the UK. No, they wished they had voted to 'Remain'.

To add insult to injury, they also told us that since one of the couple had Irish ancestry, and they would be applying for Irish passports, which would resolve their potential travel issues in Europe. For once, we were left speechless.

During this period, I continued writing articles for my usual range of newspapers and magazines, as well as for my own blog site. For a time, I decided to keep well away from the subject of Brexit, because it had become so contentious.

Whatever I wrote would please some readers, but annoy others, and so I resorted to writing about subjects that were amusing and hopefully less controversial. At this stage, I was also deeply troubled about our own future, which was now looking less than settled.

Throughout those anxious months, particularly at the end of 2018, we tried to maintain our usual range of commitments and activities. We met with friends, as usual, but conversations inevitably returned to what we would do if or when Brexit finally happened.

We usually confidently replied that, as far as we were concerned, nothing would change and that we intended to stay in our chosen country and the beautiful island of Gran Canaria for as long as possible.

Several of our friends were clearly concerned and tried to kindly warn us that this may not be the wisest of decisions, given the circumstances. They were echoing what we were beginning to suspect for ourselves.

During the year, we were happy to give homes to both an abandoned kitten, Merlin, who was discovered wandering along a busy road in the North of the island, and an unwanted and troubled dog, Oscar, who was flown over to us from Lanzarote.

Both joined our much loved, but increasingly poorly dog, Bella. Bella, at 15 years old, was beginning to show her advancing years and was now receiving treatment at a veterinary hospital on the island, after being referred there by our usual vet.

The issues relating to pet passports for our three 'fluffies', as they were collectively referred to, became of increasing concern to us, as well as to other British residents with cats and dogs.

During the early part of 2019, the issue of pet passports came to prominence. Changes to the existing pet passport scheme were due to come into effect from October that year. Additional health checks, and vaccinations would be required if we were to fly Bella, Merlin and Oscar to the UK. We knew that we were rapidly approaching decision time, and that burying our heads in the sand, hoping for a second referendum, was no longer an option.

In addition, although we were strong supporters of the Spanish health care service, which is as good if not better than that available in the UK, we also maintained private health insurance as a backup when we first moved to Spain 16 years earlier.

As it turned out, it was our private medical insurance cover that was responsible for saving my eyesight several years earlier, and which we now regarded as invaluable. We were therefore very concerned when we received a letter from our UK insurance company telling us that, due to Brexit, our medical cover would cease to be valid within Europe when the transition period began.

By February 2019, David and I had made our decision. We decided, very reluctantly, to leave Gran Canaria, which had provided us with such a happy life for most of our time living in Spain, to place our home on the market and relocate permanently to the UK.

Flying Cats and Dogs

I was grappling with bureaucracy of another dimension. I quickly discovered that credit ratings, and the power and control exercised by the UK's credit agencies had increased significantly since we had left the UK

Once David and I have made up our minds about anything, we get on with it without prevarication, fuss and excuses. We had located our new home in South Devon, and it was my role to return to deal with all manner of issues, both legal and practical relating to the new property.

David meanwhile focused upon selling our home in Gran Canaria, arranging for Bella, Merlin and Oscar's flights to the UK, the shipping of our furniture and personal effects, together with the myriad of other jobs that had to be done before we could leave the island in a sensible manner.

In addition, David was responsible for looking after the fluffies, and dealing with Bella's ongoing health issues, which were beginning to look serious.

Our new home in Devon, a bungalow, had been built in the 1950's; very little had been done since that time and the property had not been lived in for at least five years. Its once lovely, spacious garden was badly overgrown and needed serious attention.

Inside the property, there was a feeling of a home that had once been loved, but now stood still in time, and it was clear that much needed to be done before we could comfortably live there.

Despite this, it was of good, solid construction that had a great deal of potential. Over the next few weeks, I spent my time split evenly between the UK and Gran Canaria. A good contractor was recommended by our solicitor, and we were soon able to have the property rewired, central heating installed, as well as a new shower room, toilet and kitchen and new flooring, whilst I made a start on redecorating.

I seemed to live with a paintbrush permanently glued to my hand for many weeks and was relieved when that part of the work was completed. The garden, although badly overgrown, looked promising, but would need a great deal of hard work. There were many elderly shrubs and trees that needed to be removed, whilst others would need severe pruning.

Since I only arrived in the UK with a screwdriver, hammer and craft knife, I would have to wait until our stock of garden tools arrived from Gran Canaria, or I could purchase new tools from Amazon, which happened to be one of my better decisions.

Although it is currently fashionable to criticise Amazon for anything and everything, I have nothing but praise for this company. Indeed, I could not have managed without them. I had no car, and I needed a camp bed, bedding, basic kitchen items and tools to get me through the next few months.

Thankfully, items were ordered and usually delivered the following day. It was amazing that paint, cement and all manner of DIY items arrived so promptly, although it was irritating to discover a bathroom cabinet had been delivered instead of the camp bed!

For the first few days, I worked in the property during the day and returned to a hotel for a meal and to sleep at night. It was an expensive time, but a convenient option until I had a bed to sleep on.

Meanwhile in Gran Canaria, David was busy finding quotations for a removals company, which was not easy. Several of the companies that we had used in the past, or would like to use, were no longer in business, whilst others were very busy moving many other British nationals, like ourselves, who had decided to return to the UK.

Brexit certainly brought a rapid increase in business for the few removal companies on the island, and prices went up accordingly. We had to make serious decisions about how much of our furniture and personal effects we could afford to take back to the UK.

I remember that during our original move to Spain sixteen years earlier, we had to make a choice between leaving all our furniture behind, most of which had sentimental value, and had been in our families for many years, and buying new in Spain, or facing the expense of transporting our furniture to Spain.

Since we both remembered some of the cheap, tacky furniture that had adorned our various holiday apartments in Spain during earlier visits, we decide to face the expense of transportation to avoid buying new items when we arrived in Spain.

We were now faced with the same situation, but this time in reverse. Should we take the contents of our four-bedroom home in Gran Canaria back to the UK to squeeze into a two-bedroom bungalow, or buy new? In the end, we decided upon a compromise by reducing the overall quantity, which by now had been supplemented by Spanish furniture that was of rather better quality and design than British equivalents.

Beds were one good example, where Spanish beds and mattresses were far superior to those sold in the UK, despite several visits to John Lewis and other stores claiming to stock the best beds.

Eventually, we decided upon a Spanish company that worked closely with a British one, the date of the removal operation was agreed, and the deposit paid.

The only problem was that shipping from Gran Canaria to the UK would take around two months. Clearly, once in transit, David and the fluffies would immediately have to return to the UK, and we would have to camp in a basic manner in our new home until our furniture and possessions arrived in Devon.

Flying Bella, Merlin and Oscar to the UK was another serious issue to contend with. As the October deadline for the UK to leave the EU was fast approaching, and new non-EU arrangements were due to come into effect, we had to move quickly to ensure that Bella, Merlin and Oscar were out of the country before the deadline.

Again, several companies were approached for quotations, but we were very concerned to learn that we could only fly the fluffies into Heathrow, Gatwick, Manchester and Birmingham. We were even more concerned to learn that in most cases, they would have to fly to Madrid and wait for a connection to one of the named UK airports.

We could see this as a major problem, since we had heard that animals being held at Madrid Airport were not catered for particularly well, and did not have the benefit of a quiet area specifically designed for animals waiting for a connection.

Many of the flights were already fully booked for animals, since many UK nationals were faced with the same issues as us, whilst another major airline, one of only two that served the island with capacity for flying animals to the UK, was facing bankruptcy and was no longer accepting bookings for animals returning to the UK.

We even considered getting the ferry to the Spanish Peninsular and then driving Bella, Merlin and Oscar to the UK ourselves. Considering Bella's rapidly deteriorating health, we quickly dismissed that idea. This was becoming a real problem.

After many enquiries, we discovered a very helpful lady on the neighbouring island of Tenerife who said that she would sort everything out for us. She would arrange a direct flight from Gran Canaria to Manchester, a pet taxi to and from both airports, as well as an agent to deal with their collection from our home in Gran Canaria.

Upon arrival in Manchester, they would be collected by pet taxi and driven to our home in Devon the same day. Unfortunately, David would not be able to take the same flight as the fluffies, since they would arrive a week before David's departure due to the house contents removals and closure of the Gran Canaria property. It was going to be a long, tiring and stressful period for all of us; it was by no means ideal, but this was the best that we could do.

Our two cars also had to be sold. We briefly considered importing them into the UK, but quickly decided against it once we were fully informed of the expense involved. Since Brits drive 'on the wrong side of the road', as we had come to believe, the thought of driving a left-hand drive car on left side of the road was not a happy one. We had tried the same situation in reverse when we initially moved to Spain, but it was a troubling experience that we did not wish to repeat if we could avoid it.

Selling cars privately in Spain is not for the faint hearted. As a journalist, I had covered several troubling stories about cars being sold in Spain by British residents who had not done their homework.

As usual in Spain, selling and reregistering a vehicle in Spain is a time consuming, bureaucratic process. We arranged for all the paperwork connected with our transaction to be completed by an 'Asesor' in the nearby town, and someone we knew who was well used to dealing with such transactions.

The first vehicle, a Suzuki four-wheel drive, was a highly desirable vehicle on the island. Once advertised, we were inundated with calls asking to view the vehicle. Some potential purchasers arrived, made the right noises, kicked tyres, prodded and poked as prospective vehicle purchasers do, and an offer was made. The offer was far in excess of what the vehicle was worth, despite its popularity and good condition.

Something was not right; the potential buyer also declined our insistence that transferring the ownership of the car should be dealt with by our Asesor, insisting instead that we should take the vehicle to a 'colleague' of his in a town some kilometres away.

Alarm bells were already ringing, since I was currently aware of a story involving criminal activity in that area and the name of the 'colleague' mentioned also triggered a warning. Although I needed to make more enquiries, we decided to decline the offer. Subsequently, we had several increasingly angry phone calls, text messages and visits from the would-be purchaser.

It was only after threatening to call the police, as well as warning that I would be writing an article and naming him in the local newspaper, that interest in the Suzuki from this prospective purchaser ceased.

Since time was fast running out, and it was essential that both cars were sold before we left the island permanently, and we decided to sell both cars through a garage that we knew. It was a garage with an honest reputation that had been in business for many years. We vaguely knew the owner, and he seemed pleased to help us. He offered us a fair price for the Suzuki, which we agreed to.

Our much beloved Hyundai Getz was a different matter. It was already 16 years old and had been our first major purchase when we arrived in Spain 16 years earlier. This little car had acted as a temporary home for us when we moved from the Costa Banca to Gran Canaria.

It had been 'around the clock' twice, was still in very good mechanical and cosmetic condition, had never let us down; we were very reluctant to see it go. The garage owner gave us a price that I suspect was little more than scrap value, but it was time to move on. For the remainder of our time on the island, we were to be reliant on the intermittent bus service bus and taxis for the first time.

Meanwhile, back in South Devon, I was grappling with bureaucracy of another dimension. I quickly discovered that credit ratings, and the power and control exercised by the UK's credit agencies had increased significantly since we had left the UK.

Of course, consumer safety, money laundering and many other reasons are given, but first and foremost I saw it as an increasing method of government control over our lives. It was initially difficult to get water, electricity and gas connected to our property, simply because I had no credit history in the UK, despite having a UK bank account for many years.

There was a similar issue with telephone and Internet connections. I quickly managed to get around both issues by having the utilities connected in the name of the original consumer, which was the doubtful advice given to me at the time, but changed into our own names later.

We were already registered on the electoral roll, but my attempts to gain UK credit and debit cards were initially rejected, simply because I had not lived in the UK for the required minimum of three years; the fact that I had lived, worked and paid taxes for several decades earlier seemed to have no relevance.

Fortunately, I had a selection of Spanish credit and debit cards that I could use in the UK, until our UK bank agreed to issue us with their own cards, which took several months.

The purchase of a new car in the UK was a relatively simple matter, since our experiences with the Hyundai Getz meant that the decision for our new car was already made, it would be another Hyundai.

The purchase of motoring insurance was an obstacle that I had not even considered. Having achieved an accident-free motoring history in both the UK and Spain, I assumed that my full no claims discount from the Spanish insurer would be transferred to a UK insurance, particularly as it was the same company - Linea Directa in Spain and Direct Line in the UK. This was not to be the case, since both insurers are owned by different companies and "We don't do things like that".

Instead, I had to purchase a motoring insurance policy, without a no claims discount, which was expensive, although I was cheerfully told that I would get a ten per cent discount if I remained accident free the following year. I duly changed insurance companies, which made me feel a little better, particularly when I was offered a 20 per cent "goodwill discount" and a free rucksack if I joined them.

Improvements were being carried out in our bungalow at a rapid pace, which was just as well, since Bella, Merlin and Oscar would soon be flying into the UK.

I made one of my last visits to Gran Canaria and was shocked to see how much our beloved Bella had deteriorated in the short time since I had last seen her. Her significant health issues were compounded by the fact that she could now barely see or walk. I think I was more aware of the sudden deterioration in Bella's health and general mobility, as I had been away from her for several weeks.

It was now quite clear to me that it would not be fair to fly Bella to a new country and a new home, and as heart-breaking as it was, it was time to say goodbye. As anyone who has lived with and loved a dog, cat or any animal will know, this is one of the most difficult decisions to make. Despite our distress, we had to put Bella first; she would always be our very special Spanish girl.

It was August, and the day of Merlin and Oscar's flight to the UK. I had bought new beds, bowls and all manner of accessories that Merlin and Oscar were used to, since their items would not be delivered from Gran Canaria for a couple of months.

As ludicrous as it may sound, Manchester was the only way that we could get them to South Devon. It was a day that both David and I were dreading. Merlin and Oscar were placed in suitable crates, collected by pet taxi and checked in at Las Palmas Airport. The courier waited with them until they had boarded their flights and we monitored their flight closely on our mobile phone flight app.

Once their flight arrived in Manchester, there would be veterinary checks at the airport before Merlin and Oscar were released to the pet taxi. It was a very long drive from Manchester to South Devon, but I reasoned that maybe the traffic wouldn't be too bad at that time of night, despite it being holiday season and the M5 was notorious for delays, accidents and all manner of problems. Even so, I could not see Merlin and Oscar arriving until the following morning.

It was just before midnight when I heard a van pull up outside our front gate. Yes, it was the pet taxi! The driver confirmed that all had gone smoothly, and Merlin and Oscar didn't have too long to wait before they were released from their checks at the airport.

Two crates were carefully lifted out of the taxi and lifted into the kitchen. Oscar immediately dashed outside his crate and gave me a welcome that I will never forget. He was clearly very hungry and after his initial enthusiastic welcome, looked around the kitchen for his food.

He quickly found it and devoured it with relish before falling asleep in his new bed, clearly exhausted. Merlin, on the other hand, was very subdued, and as I carefully lifted him out of his much smaller crate, I could see that he was very distressed.

I lifted him onto the new sofa in the living room, and he immediately jumped off and hid behind a cupboard. As those who know cats will appreciate, they like to settle on their own terms, and fuss is best avoided until they come to terms with their new surroundings.

I was very concerned about him, and began to wonder if we had made the right decision in flying Merlin to the UK? Maybe, we should have considered his welfare more and rehomed him with friends on the island?

53

Merlin would not eat or drink for several days. This concerned me greatly, since we had already lost our cat, Mac, two years earlier; he would not eat and deteriorated very quickly.

I tried as many brands and varieties of cat food that I could find, as well as treats such as cheese that I thought would encourage Merlin to start responding. Eventually, I found a new, and very expensive cat food in the local pet store, which I bought. I poured a little into Merlin's new bowl, he walked towards the bowl, sniffed briefly, and eventually took a small piece of food and hid.

It smelt disgusting, but Merlin clearly appreciated it. From that moment, Merlin began to eat and drink enthusiastically. He was clearly very hungry and thirsty, but he began to behave in his usual way and was very pleased when he was reunited with Oscar. It was a troubling few days.

Meanwhile in Gran Canaria, David was winding down our responsibilities on the island and was rapidly clearing the house. Sadly, although we were keen gardeners in Gran Canaria, we had to leave all our plants behind. It was sad to leave some of our special garden plants, and my collection of orchids, which were given away to friends and neighbours.

Other unwanted items were collected by two of our favourite charity shops. Unlike in the UK, these charities cheerfully accepted anything offered to them, without any complaints of items not being good enough.

The removals company arrived and spent two days wrapping and packing our lives into a large container. There was only just enough space in the container for all our belongings, and David had to make the decision to leave several items behind if we were to avoid additional shipping costs.

David spent his final night in our home on a small camp bed in our now empty living room before an early start the following day. He was collected by taxi and taken to the airport before saying a final goodbye to an island that had been our home for the last sixteen years. He took with him endless happy memories that would never be forgotten.

Later that afternoon, I collected a weary looking David from the railway station. It was his first time in the UK for several years, and initially he appeared bewildered by what he was experiencing as we walked the short distance from the railway station.

Once David entered the bungalow and was given a rapturous welcome by Oscar and a more grudging welcome by Merlin, he commented that it already felt like home. At last, after a very difficult few months, the four of us were reunited.

There was no doubt that, for us, 2019 was a very difficult year. Those readers who are of the Brexit persuasion will no doubt be irritated that I place much of the blame for our sudden return to the UK upon an irrational, ill-considered vote that was supported by false claims and misinformation.

Time will tell. Despite this, I have no doubt that even without Brexit we would, one day, have decided to return to the UK, but based upon our own decision and when we felt that the time was right for us.

It is true to say that whilst living in Gran Canaria we missed our family and friends, although many of our friends visited Gran Canaria regularly on holiday and would spend time with us. We always looked forward to these visits and enjoyed their company.

Our return to the UK and a new home in South Devon has been broadly successful although, in contrast, we missed our Spanish friends, lifestyle and, of course, the climate.

To confuse matters even further, shortly after our return to the UK, Covid 19 burst into our lives and we were all faced with lockdowns and a rapid change in the way that we manage our lives. In the next few chapters of this book, I hope to contrast some of our new experiences in the UK with our lives in Gran Canaria; the experiences that I will describe are neither good nor bad, just different.

Not Good, Not Bad, Just Different

The lady clerk in the Devon council office could learn a great deal from her colleagues working on a small island in the Atlantic.

Our first few weeks living in our new home in the UK were initially very challenging. The bungalow aside, one of the many things that I was looking forward to experiencing when we moved to the UK was the Waitrose supermarket. Sadly, the experience did not last long.

Waitrose was a supermarket that I had a lot of respect for and longed to shop in once again from the time that we last lived in the UK. It was not the kind of supermarket that we could, at that time, afford to shop in regularly for our weekly groceries, but it was the kind of supermarket that had treats and surprises that we could not get elsewhere.

As vegetarians, it seemed that Waitrose was one of the very few supermarkets that understood what most vegetarians look for. Most vegetarians do not need vegetarian food dressed up as "chicken flavour" or "beef flavour", but a product that looked and tasted nothing like meat.

It always amused us when we saw "vegetarian bacon" advertised in another supermarket; most self-respecting vegetarians and vegans would want nothing to do with such a foolishly named product.

Our move to Spain sixteen years earlier was not an easy one for vegetarians. I am convinced that at the time most Spanish people regarded tuna as a vegetable, and that most vegetarians would be happy to eat it sprinkled over their salad, which surely tasted too bland without it?

Similarly, those delicious Spanish omelettes, which never taste the same when cooked out of the country, should contain potato, and possibly onion if feeling particularly adventurous.

Sadly, many Spanish restaurants believed that adding a dash of ham would liven up the dish considerably and surely please their new English clients? If they complain, just tell them that the red pieces are red pepper, and the problem will go away; we experienced a number of variations on this theme.

Although Spain is awash with delicious fruit and vegetables at all times of the year, the opportunity to buy vegetarian ready-made meals in supermarkets was virtually impossible when we first arrived in Spain.

One of our favourite supermarkets was a large chain called Mercadonna. This supermarket was generally good value and could usually be relied upon to provide a good range of fresh fruit and vegetables.

On the other hand, there was another large supermarket chain, Carrefour, that spanned much of Europe. This supermarket carried a larger and much more imaginative stock of fruit and vegetables, but was a supermarket that we avoided during the summer months, since their fresh produce deteriorated far too quickly. Unlike Mercadonna, the temperature inside the store was always far too high for fruit and vegetables to survive for long.

Back in Devon, I was enjoying time spent in a UK supermarket once again. In Waitrose, particularly, I was tempted with all manner of fresh produce and, best of all, prepared ready meals. Initially living on my own in the new property before David could join me, I was so busy throughout those very long days cleaning, painting and repairing that I had little time to prepare meals.

In any case, all I had available was a kettle, electric toaster and a microwave oven; even the gas cooker that I had retained from the house clearance had died. I would escape the daily chaos by walking the short distance to Waitrose where I could browse for a ready meal and then enjoy a coffee and cake in the café before returning 'home' to the chaos that was waiting for me.

For several weeks, it was a welcome escape that I valued. There was even a free supply of coffee for those that purchased one of their special mugs!

I also liked my local Waitrose store, since they seemed to have a very good policy that supported the local community. One example of this was the large collection of recycling skips located in their car park. This was very useful for me, since at the beginning of my relocation to the town, I did not have the necessary range of coloured boxes and bins that indicated that one was accepted as a 'true resident'.

There were black bins, green bins, blue containers for food waste, blue bags for newspapers and magazines, green boxes and black boxes. I really did not understand what these were for, how to use them and when they were emptied. I decided to have a chat with a friendly neighbour, who was very helpful, sat me down with a coffee, and explained which box was used for what, and when they were due to be emptied; it was all very confusing.

In Gran Canaria, we did not have local refuse collections. There was a large hopper close to the seafront where we would take our rubbish each day, and there were others scattered around the village, each close to a local community of properties.

Each hopper was also an electric crusher which, in theory, would be activated once or twice a day that would allow more rubbish to be comfortably stored until it was emptied by a large collection vehicle.

The system generally worked very well until the usual collection of saints' days, holidays and staff illness punctuated the usual routine. Then the huge hopper would then sit, not activated, for several days, giving off disgusting smells and providing a breeding ground for flies, locusts and welcome treats for rats, as well as stray dogs and cats.

One afternoon, when I called in the store to buy my evening meal, I stopped at the café and found one of the usually cheerful members of staff in tears. I had spoken to Sarah several times before; she was a local woman and had been very helpful in giving me advice about where I could buy this or that, and asked her what the matter was.

She told me that they had just heard that Waitrose was closing the store. I was shocked to hear this and sympathised with Sarah. I knew that the John Lewis Partnership usually had an impressive record of looking after their staff, or 'partners' as they are called, and asked Sarah if she had been offered a job at one of their other stores, which were not too far away.

"That's the problem," she sobbed, "they are closing the other local stores as well; there's nothing left in this area for us."

Indeed, they did close the supermarket, as well as most of the other branches in the area. It happened very quickly and was a distressing time for the staff who had given loyalty and service and, in some cases, for many years.

I missed my short walk to buy my meal and the friendly chat and helpful advice from the staff. I also missed the large recycling hoppers that suddenly disappeared with no mention of where they would be resituated. I hadn't quite realised at the time, but this was going to be an issue for me.

During my first weeks in our new home, I had no means of transport and therefore ordered all the necessary items online from Amazon and other online companies. As most readers will be aware, products ordered in this way are accompanied by huge amounts of packaging. I had ordered furniture, paint, step ladders, shelves, timber amongst many other large items that came, usually well wrapped, in large boxes.

Very soon, our large garage was nearly full of folded cartons that had to be disposed of. One day I called the local council for assistance and was put through to a less than helpful member of staff. I asked if someone could visit to collect the cardboard boxes, as well as the faulty gas cooker.

"No, we don't do that. You will have to take the boxes to your local recycling point."

I asked where such a point was and was told that it was in the Waitrose car park. I mentioned that they had been taken away following the closure of the store.

"You'll just have to take them to another recycling point then, won't you?" came the curt reply.

I pointed out that I had no transport.

"Fold them up, stand on them if you have to, and put them in the recycling box." She sighed.

With my patience wearing thin, I repeated that I had a garage full of boxes, and they would not fit into one small recycling box, however much I stamped on them.

"Spread it over a few weeks then. By the way, we can take your gas cooker."

Good news at last. I asked when it could be collected?

"You must give us at least four weeks' notice, and it will cost forty pounds. Just leave it outside your door, but you'll have to buy a permit first."

With that, I politely declined the offer, looked in the local paper and discovered a very helpful man called Vince. Vince arrived the following day with George, and both men cheerfully emptied the garage, cleared away unwanted rocks, bricks and all manner of rubbish from the garden, together with the gas cooker, all for forty pounds.

I had been warned by a neighbour to make sure that I asked to see a recycling licence from anyone collecting rubbish from our property, since fly tipping was a problem in the area. With the unhelpful attitude of the local council that I had experienced, I could now fully understand why fly tipping was a serious and growing problem.

In Gran Canaria, recycling was never an issue. As I mentioned earlier, as well as the main rubbish hoppers, there were also recycling bins for clothing, shoes, cardboard, plastic etc, which worked well. In addition, charity shops were always willing to accept items offered to them, and most would cheerfully collect larger items.

The town council would often surprisingly quickly collect large, unwanted, broken items such cookers, fridges and beds. Some of these items would be repaired for use, even on a temporary basis, by homeless people and the many asylum seekers that were now arriving in Spain from the Western Sahara.

Looking back, their policy was both responsible and sensible; fly tipping was never an issue. The lady clerk in the Devon council office could learn a great deal from her colleagues working on a small island in the Atlantic.

Our local Waitrose supermarket was eventually turned into a Lidl supermarket. Without being too disparaging about the store, as I know many people like it and the good value that it offers, it is not a store that I use very often.

The fruit and vegetables are usually excellent, but I rarely recognise some of the brands that appear briefly before they disappear for ever. I find it very hard to have any kind of loyalty to a supermarket that proudly claims as its slogan "When it's gone, it's gone". Sadly, the recycling bins never reappeared either.

Taking Back Control ... With Flags

The UK is governed by a motley collection of unelected peers, grandees, occasional Russian oligarchs and other worthies in the House of Lords, and a distorted voting system that provides the House of Commons with Members of Parliament that are not based upon proportional representation.

I have never really understood the reasoning behind this often-used slogan of the campaign to leave the European Union.

Clearly, leaving the European Union did not mean "taking back control" when the country is governed by a motley collection of unelected peers, grandees, occasional Russian oligarchs and other worthies in the House of Lords, and a distorted voting system that provides the House of Commons with Members of Parliament that are not based upon proportional representation.

The point that sharing a degree of sovereignty with other nations meant that all constituent nations in the EU had a say in how the organisation should be run, but was usually and conveniently ignored.

Do you remember that superb Observer series of pocket size books containing all manner of useful information? The series covered many topic areas, but one that I remember giving me a lot of pleasure as a child was 'The Observer Book of Flags'. I remember leafing through those colourful, glossy pages, trying to find the countries that the flag represented in an atlas.

Later, my fascination with flags and the countries that they represented led me to collect stamps. I would spend hours examining these tiny works of art, marvelling at the exotic birds and animals featured on many of the more artistic creations, whilst wondering whether some of the very important people featured, usually unsmiling, on the stamps of other, no doubt more serious, nations were really that important.

When we moved to Spain, and later to the Canary Islands, flags were an important and interesting feature. Each of the islands had their own flag, and it was interesting to see how these, and other flags were displayed and used. As a reporter, I would attend all manner of conferences, meetings, openings of building and events. Each of these events always had three flags as a backdrop, the flag of the Canary Islands, the Spanish flag, and the European Union flag.

I noticed this phenomenon particularly because of the sharp contrast to such events in the UK. Similar events in the UK rarely displayed any flag at all. Any project, such as bridges, roads as well as many smaller projects that the European Union had funded in the Canary Islands would always display a notice of explanation about the European Union's contribution to the project.

In the UK, substantial funding provided by the EU to major infrastructure projects were generally ignored; there was rarely a mention, let alone a display of the European Union flag. The result of this, in my view, deliberate omission, led to the British public being left unaware of the European Union's contribution to the UK, whilst Spanish and other European citizens were usually much better informed.

Flags can also be very destructive; as well as encouraging nationalism, they can also foster jingoism and hate. We see this at wartime, as well as during football matches.

Many will of course say that these two extremes are an overreaction and that there is nothing intrinsically wrong in having 'pride' in your country and football team, represented by a flag. I would counter this by asking what exactly is the basis of pride in one's country or team? Did you score a goal for your team or contributed in a unique way to your country and its people? Generally, the answer is no, and 'pride' is based purely on reflected glory.

Basically, flags encourage a sense of unity to a common cause, but at the expense of a dislike of others who do not share the same flag and accompanying beliefs. In recent years, the sight of the union flag and the English flag have made me shudder. I have noticed many more union and English flags flying since our return to the UK.

Some have rightly been flown to commemorate events during the two World Wars, and to recognise the sacrifices made by so many servicemen for their country. Others, such as the English flag, displaying the cross of St George, have been adopted as symbols of power by right wing groups, such as the British National Party, and other neo fascist groups.

Returning to the UK and seeing so many English and union flags fluttering from buildings in towns is a phenomenon that I have not seen in the UK before. This sudden affection to both flags appears to be the result of the many arguments and divided opinions both before and after the vote to leave the European Union.

Strangely, the flying of these flags did not appear to be used in celebration, but more one of defiance. The flags had become a rallying cry of support to a cause of 'Us against Them'. I guess that few could articulate exactly what cause their flag flying was celebrating, given that the UK had already left the European Union and their cause had supposedly been won.

Maybe the flags were being used as a kind of grown up 'comfort blanket' to reassure that all would be well? Would those nasty Remainers try to overturn their deeply held belief of 'Taking back control'?

Returning to the UK in February 2019, I was struck by what I saw as a very troubled and divided country.

Despite the vote that was supposed to settle matters 'once and for all', and the election of a right-wing government and Prime Minister with a significant majority, long held arguments and divisions continued.

I have my doubts that many people who have lived through these troubled times are aware of how much the UK has changed in recent years. For others who have been out of the country for a long time, the change in attitudes is stark.

Attitudes to those in need, asylum seekers and foreigners are now much harsher than in previous times. I quickly learned to avoid mentioning Spain and Europe and our life within the context of the European Union to strangers!

I grew up in a part of rural Lincolnshire that I detested. I could not leave the area fast enough in my late teenage years to join the civil service in Bournemouth. This area, known as Holland, was flat, uninspiring and always seemed to smell of rotting cabbages, or worse. Other parts of Lincolnshire were much more scenic and a pleasure to visit.

After all, this was the area where many of the nation's crops were grown and harvested. As a result, this basic exploitation of acres of cheap land led to generations of well-off farmers. Most had a comfortable, sustainable living, whilst others were extremely rich.

Over the years, farms and land were merged to create huge mechanically reliant enterprises. The days of the comfortable small holder were long gone, and it was the industrial farm that was seen as the future.

One of the main problems with these farms was that there was a shortage of workers willing to pick and harvest crops, work in the abattoirs, food processing plants and canning factories. There was a growing reliance upon workers from Europe and willing workers from Poland and Romania, to name just two countries where recruitment was relatively simple.

The wealthy farm owners were happy, as they could appoint and dismiss workers as they pleased. They could pay low wages, enjoy the benefits of non-unionised labour whilst providing the most basic of accommodation. Some would later describe the working conditions and general exploitation of these workers as a form of slave labour.

As time went on, many of these European workers decided to stay in the country, bring families to join them, as well as forming relationships with local people. They tended to settle in groups within towns, such as the small market town of Boston, which quickly became renowned as a centre for the Polish community.

The Poles brought wealth, new ideas, different foods and music to the town, but naturally continued to speak in their own language when together. This quickly led to resentment and division. In Boston, we can see a microcosm of the development of an 'anti-foreigner' viewpoint for which membership of the European Union was to be blamed.

In reality, of course, it was the greed of the Lincolnshire landowners, low wages and poor working conditions that led to the reluctance of British workers to toil on the land and factories that was the real issue. Despite propaganda to the contrary, it was not the willingness of European workers to work hard and try to make a life for themselves in another country that was the issue.

Growing up in a narrow-minded rural community, such as this part of Lincolnshire, I was grateful that my parents brought me up to have a much more enlightened attitude towards Europe from my early teens. I am still surprised that they agreed for me to take part in an exchange visit to stay with a family in Germany, as part of a school exchange programme, when I was thirteen years old. I was to stay with a family in Germany for two weeks with a German boy, called Karl, of about the same age.

The following year, Karl stayed with us in Lincolnshire. This was my first visit to another country and gave me a rich, unforgettable experience that shaped my early views of another country. It gave me a brief glimpse of what life outside the confines of the Lincolnshire village was like.

There were people from another culture, speaking another language, studying, working and living who were much like as me. Many decades later, I am still in regular contact with Karl and his family, and this experience played a significant part of my early education and ignited my love and appreciation of Europe.

Looking back, I now realise that my parents had very open-minded views about Europe. My father was a hospital administrator and superintendent of a hospital and children's home in Lincolnshire, and my mother was the matron of both establishments.

During the war, four German prisoners of war were billeted at the hospital, and worked in the gardens and carried out general porterage duties. Although this was long before I was born, my parents would speak fondly of the four young, German men.

They would tell of the times that they had enjoyed a meal together; one was a brilliant musician and would entertain the group playing my mother's piano. One of the men regularly acted as a babysitter for my elder brother when my parents were working.

These men were talented carpenters and artists, and often they would carve toys made from wood for my brother. My father would give them scraps of wood and paint that he found and bought them a cheap set of artists paints and brushes. The four men spoke excellent English and they quickly became trusted friends with my parents.

There were tearful farewells when these men finally returned to their homeland, and my parents kept in contact with them for several years. We still have a beautifully constructed and painted fireguard of a woodland bridge and a superb painting of a yellow rose in our family - gifts presented by the German prisoners of war when they final left Lincolnshire.

I still recall the words of my father when he spoke about their time together, "We never once discussed the war; there was no need. Those men were not our enemies, just good men with families like us who were dragged into war by their leaders who should have known better."

I have often felt that these words, together with my visit to Germany formed the basis of my future relationship with Europe, and I am grateful for it.

I often wonder if the general British suspicion of 'foreigners' is a residual effect of the two World Wars? The 'let's smash them' mentality, together with the ignorance and jingoism displayed so effectively during football matches against European clubs that makes me wonder if it is partly a remnant of the 'We won the war and the 1966 cup final' mentality that is to blame for Brexit?

Basically, it is playground aggression at its worst. Often, writers blame Britain's isolated island culture, over glorified stories of the days of Empire, and Britain's role in the two world wars for much of its present-day arrogance in world affairs.

To this broad analysis, I would add that a lack of an enlightened European education, together with the teaching of European languages from an early age, the lack of opportunities or willingness to travel, live and work with people from other cultures has led to an anti-European feeling within many of the British public.

As I write this, there is intense fighting between Russia and Ukraine, and I have been struck with not only the compassion and concern shown by many in the UK towards those killed or injured in the conflict, but with many families offering accommodation in their homes for Ukrainian refugees. There is also a surprising willingness, albeit with initial, sheepish reluctance, of UK ministers to work with colleagues across Europe in seeking a peaceful resolution to this unfolding tragedy.

It is noticeable that many observers comment that being a member of the EU would have made decision making more effective if the UK was still at "the heart of Europe" rather than an outsider seeking to join major decision making. It is almost laughable to see Johnson scurrying around Europe in his bid to be seen as another wartime Churchill when, in reality, he is mostly irrelevant.

As regular readers of my articles will be aware, I have always wanted, and still wish, to be part of the European Union, or as close as we can get, given the current Brexit fiasco. As I have tried to explain, this is not only for cultural and emotional reasons, but for clear economic reasons too.

It was Margaret Thatcher, not my favourite politician, who staunchly promoted and defended the foundation of a single market as well as close cooperation with our European neighbours. Negotiating the single market in 1987 was often considered Thatcher's greatest free trade achievement and was widely regarded as being in both Britain's and Europe's interest; it was a great success.

I am sure that this was not due to Thatcher's fondness for Europe in general, but sensible recognition that it would be in the best interests of Britain, financially, as well as to foster improvements in trade, security and increased influence in the world by working and cooperating. Later, Johnson reversed that achievement in what is increasingly seen as an act of naked political ambition. The pretence that it was necessary for Brexit to be successful was his biggest lie.

Damage created by our departure is becoming increasing clear to all. At the time of writing, we have a perfect storm of issues that could have been avoided, with the disruption of flows of global trade and a shortage of drivers, which has been made worse by both the pandemic, Brexit and Russia's war with Ukraine.

Maybe there is no such thing as "Taking Back Control", and it really is just about flag waving, 'Ya boo' politics and poor playground behaviour after all?

Expats and Immigrants

Over the years, I have come to realise that the term 'expat' is a remnant of British Colonial days and sounds entitled, if not plain arrogant.

As with most people, I have some regrets in life and sometimes think of ways that I could have done things a little differently. One of my regrets is using the term 'expat' in many of my articles and books. Over the years, I have come to realise that the term 'expat' is a remnant of British Colonial days and sounds entitled, if not plain arrogant.

Why is it that the British living overseas continue to call themselves by this title? There are thousands of British 'expats' in Spain, France, Greece and Italy, and I am quite sure that few of them will refer to themselves as British 'immigrants', although this is what they truly are.

So, what and who is an 'expat'? A quick glimpse on Wikipedia helpfully reveals that an expatriate, which is usually shortened to 'expat', is a person temporarily or permanently residing in a country other than that of the person's upbringing.

The word comes from the Latin term ex (out of) and patria (country, fatherland). You would think that, given this definition, anyone living outside of their home country for a length of time could be described as an 'expat', irrespective of colour or skin colour, but this is not the case. The term is used exclusively for western people, with white skins, living and working abroad.

Asians are immigrants, Arabs are immigrants and Africans are immigrants, but Europeans are expats simply because they choose to be superior. Immigrants is a colonial term reserved for 'inferior races'. Clearly this view is both racist and wrong is so many ways.

This issue was made abundantly clear to me one morning as I was taking our dog, Bella, for a walk along the seafront, when I saw a small, roughly made boat, called a 'patera' being pulled to shore by four men. There were several police officers closely observing, and Red Cross staff were running across the beach towards the patera; I stood watching the unfolding drama.

The small boat contained about ten men and women and four small children. One of the women was holding a baby tightly in her arms. As the men dragged the patera onto the beach, they were soon assisted by Red Cross staff and the police officers.

The men were clearly exhausted; they wore no shoes, carried no belongings and their clothes looked dirty and well worn. Two of the men fell to the ground as soon as they reached dry land. Police officers and Red Cross Staff gently helped the women and children from the patera and guided them towards the Red Cross vehicle. Two of the children were carried by police officers and all were immediately wrapped in thick blankets and given a bottle of water.

This was the first time that I had witnessed an actual landing of immigrants, no doubt from the Western Sahara, even though I had covered the story of these landings many times as a reporter. I had seen beaches on the island littered with these small, roughly made boats, which looked most unseaworthy, but somehow, they managed to cross the Atlantic to the islands.

What I had just witnessed was very emotional; I saw the desperation, fear and exhaustion in the faces of these people. The despair that these people must feel to risk their lives and that of their children on such a dangerous journey to a country that they did not know is difficult to comprehend.

Presumably, these people were not only escaping war and persecution, but also seeking a better life. As I have often said, it is only an accident of birth that places us where we are and the circumstances that we find ourselves.

I continued my walk with Bella, who was now getting very impatient to continue her walk. As I walked away from this tragic glimpse of life, I gave thanks that at least they had safely arrived on the island and wished them well.

It was later that day David and I wandered with Bella to our favourite café bar on the sea front. After a busy morning, we would often find ourselves in this friendly bar and enjoy a glass of wine and papas arugadas (small potatoes, boiled in salt water, served with a delicious mojo sauce).

It was an ideal way to relax, and the sparkling blue sea and cloudless sky made for an unforgettable backdrop. As we were enjoying our drinks, we spotted another British couple who lived in the adjacent road to ourselves. We knew the couple vaguely, but they were not a couple with whom we would wish to develop a friendship.

Helen, a noisy, bossy woman in her mid 50s, seemed to delight in speaking sharply to her partner, Peter. Peter was a frail looking older man with whom I had had several conversations during my morning walks with Bella. He seemed pleasant enough, but troubled.

After meeting his wife during a recent public meeting, I could understand why he looked troubled. Helen waved cheerfully in our direction, and we waved back, desperately hoping that they did not join us at our table.

"Mind if we join you?" beamed Helen, as she plonked her large frame in the seat beside me. We could not refuse, since the café bar was almost full, and we were the only remaining table with two spare seats.

"No, of course not," I replied, beckoning Peter to the other seat. "Isn't it a glorious day? Have you just come back from a walk?"

"I just had to get out of the house. Peter's been drilling holes in walls and banging away all morning. I just had to get out of the house; I felt one of my heads coming on."

"Oh, what has he been doing?" asked David, looking at Peter, who had just ordered large two gin and tonics."

"I'm fitting shelving. Helen's been on about it since we moved. Now, I have finally got around to it, she's still not happy," replied Peter, glaring at his wife, who sniffed loudly and looked away.

We thought the safest thing to do was to change the subject, but Helen started speaking before I could open my mouth.

"Have you heard the news? Isn't it awful?"

As I was at that time one of the few purveyors of news on the island, I thought it highly unlikely that anything untoward had happened since we had left our home.

"No, what do you mean?"

"Those awful illegals again! Do you know a boat full of them landed in our village this morning? Over there, just a few yards away," said Helen, with a voice of disgust, waving in the direction of the sad little patera that I had seen earlier.

"Yes, I was there when it landed this morning. It was a very sad sight to see such desperate people. Why do you call them illegals? We don't know that they are."

Helen sniffed and glared at me. "Of course, they are illegal immigrants. Why else would they be here and arrive secretly when they think no one is looking. All they want is to be given free accommodation and welfare paid by the state. It's us that will be paying for them. Anyway, the men are most likely terrorists."

"That's a sweeping statement, Helen. They may be asylum seekers coming through the Western Sahara, seeking help and safety. They have children with them too. Why do you say they are terrorists?"

Helen extended herself to her full seated height, looking angry. "They have no right to be here. They will be Muslim and most of them are terrorists. I feel sorry for the women though. That's no way to live, dressed like that."

There was silence. I had plenty of words that I wanted to say, but felt that in the spirit of good neighbourliness, I should let these foolish remarks pass. Finally, I could hold my thoughts no longer.

"Why did you and Peter move here, Helen?"

"For the sunshine, a healthier lifestyle and cheap booze," replied Helen without a second thought. "What about you and David? Same, I guess."

"For a healthier and happier life in the sun," I replied, "Don't you think that a better life is what these people are after too? After all, we are all immigrants."

"Rubbish," exclaimed Helen loudly. "I am not an immigrant, we are expats, and proud of it. We pay our taxes; we have papers, and we have every right to live here as we are part of the European Union. No, we are expats and certainly not immigrants," she sniffed.

Peter, who had been listening in silence, suddenly spoke up. "He's got a point, Helen. We are immigrants, but we call ourselves expats. Why?

Helen, who was now looking quite pink almost shouted at her husband. "We are nothing like those people. We have a right to be here. We are legal, they are not. We contribute to the country, we obey the laws, and we are not terrorists!"

It was at that point that we could stand the conversation with this bigoted woman no longer. We made our usual excuse of needing to return home to feed Bella, and quickly left the café bar.

Despite the anger that I felt following this unpleasant, unintelligent conversation, I was grateful that Peter had attempted to express his thoughts about the unreasonableness of his wife's argument.

Sadly, I realised that what Helen had said was the view that I had heard expressed by others many times, albeit more calmly considered and argued. I began to question my own views about what I meant by using the term 'expat' and not 'immigrant' in my writing.

I claimed to myself that my usage of the term was innocent enough, but I also realised that my own view and usage of the term was based upon ignorance and some laziness.

It is true that in my writing, British people immediately relate to the term, 'expat', but I made a pledge on that day, to avoid using the term 'expat' in future.

I would also attempt to change the titles of several earlier publications should they ever be republished. As for Helen and Peter, I understand that they could no longer face living in our Canarian village and had returned to their home in Folkstone.

Wickedly, we have been wondering how they now feel about the dozens of immigrants crossing the Channel from France each day. Sadly, I doubt that Helen has learned anything from her experiences in the Canary Islands, although I had learned something valuable from them.

Police and Crime

The next tier of police is the Guardia Civil, who often used to be referred to unkindly as 'Franco's Thugs'. These are a paramilitary police force, usually housed in secure local barracks. They are effective, no nonsense and often harsh in their methods, but they get the job done.

In the three years that we have lived in South Devon, I have not seen a police officer in the town or on the seafront. Maybe they are lurking there somewhere, hiding or in disguise, but their presence is never visible. I have heard several police cars zooming past the road where we live, sirens blaring and presumably on their way to an incident.

On one occasion, we were visited by a friendly police community officer who gave us a helpful leaflet and sticker about 'cold callers' and she kindly advised us what to do if we were troubled by them. Our most common police presence are police helicopters hovering overhead, often searching for someone lost at sea.

I remember a few years ago when we were making a brief visit to the UK to see our family, that we stopped for a break in the county town of Dorchester. We went to the public conveniences, which is where I discovered a wallet on the floor.

When I opened it, I could see from the driving licence that the wallet belonged to an elderly man. It contained a substantial amount of cash, as well as credit and debit cards.

We were anxious to continue our journey, as we still had a good way to travel, but decided to find the local police station and leave the wallet there. We found the police station, but were disappointed to discover that it was only open for three mornings each week.

There was a telephone number to call, but there was no letter box for us to drop off the wallet. I could hear people talking and laughing inside the building, but despite knocking on the door, no one answered.

We decided to call the telephone contact number and was informed that the nearest police station that could help was at Winfrith, which was some miles away, and "no" they could not arrange to collect the wallet. In the end we decided to drive to the address on the driving licence ourselves.

We discovered the elderly man, who was in a considerable state of distress at having lost his wallet, being comforted by one of his neighbours. I will never forget the joy expressed by the elderly man when he realised that we had come to return his wallet fully intact to him.

It was then that I first became concerned about the UK's police service and aware of the lack of support in times of crisis. I contrast this early experience of police and crime in the UK to our life in Spain and the Canary Islands. Our first experience was living in the Costa Banca for two years.

We had moved into an attractive, small, detached villa within an urbanisation inhabited mainly by British people, Germans, Swedish and Belgians, but very few Spanish. It was not quite what we were looking for when moving to Spain, but it did give us a good foundation for our new life in the country, particularly since nearly everyone spoke English and we were still struggling with the language.

When we moved into our new property, our neighbours, who were always very kind and helpful, were insistent that we take security very seriously. The property already had metal 'prison like bars' on all the windows (they were not as unattractive as it might sound) and we immediately had a very solid, metal door fitted. This heavy metal door was very similar to that fitted to a bank vault, so I suspect knocking down a wall to gain access would have been easier than trying to gain access through that door.

In addition, a sophisticated alarm system was installed, and we had all walls surrounding the property raised and electrically controlled driveway gates installed. We also added a sign to the front gate, which said 'Perros peligrosso' (dangerous dogs). Later, we were told that it was this sign that saved the day.

It was our dogs, Barney and Bella, who appeared to be our main security system. Barney, a stubborn but loveable corgi with a very impressive, deep bark, and Bella, a short-tempered Spanish girl with very sharp teeth who did not take prisoners, who acted as our first line of defence.

Crime rates were high in the area and the Russian Mafia were often to blame. Their spread seemed to reach everywhere through drug trafficking, prostitution, guns and people smuggling, as well as low level crime.

Indeed, it was an article that I wrote as a new, inexperienced and naïve reporter that got me into serious trouble with the Russian Mafia on one occasion. I won't go into detail of the incident here, but suffice to say that I was very grateful when we were posted to the Canary Islands a few weeks later.

By the time that we left the Costa Blanca two years later, we were the only people in our road who had not been burgled. Our neighbours were convinced that it was the 'Perros Pelegrosso' sign and Barney and Bella's determined security efforts that had helped, and less to do with our expensive security measures.

Indeed, on the day that we left the Costa Blanca for our new life in the Canary Islands, our next-door neighbours had been robbed. The couple were chloroformed in their sleep; by the time that they awoke, all their possessions were gone.

When we returned to the UK, we were immediately faced with the election of local council officials, as well as voting for another official that I was completely unaware of, that of the Police and Crime Commissioner (PCC). It seems that the PCC was a new, political construct designed to make the police more accountable to the general public.

Over the years, I have learned as a reporter, never to take things at face value, but to investigate, ask searching questions, and find out more. My research revealed that not only are PCCs a political appointment, but they are also paid handsomely and have a large team of support staff to assist them with their no doubt onerous duties.

I had always thought that the Chief Constable of a police force was the person best placed to decide priorities for their area, as well as acting as the main interface between the police service and the general public. I am told that this is 'old fashioned thinking ' and that electing a PCC is the way forward. I remain unconvinced, but I voted for one anyway, still wondering how many more police officers could be recruited with the salary paid to the PCC and their staff?

We always felt very safe in the Canary Islands, in contrast to the Costa Blanca. When we moved into our new home on the island, there were no bars on any windows although we did have our security alarm transferred and fitted to our new home.

When our new next-door neighbour saw the alarm, he looked puzzled. "Why did you have alarm fitted? It is no necessary here", he asked in broken English. I explained where we had come from and the issues that we had faced.

Juan Carlos nodded and smiled, "No problem here. I leave door unlocked. If I not here, you need something, go and take it and give it back later. Ok?" This was a refreshing and welcoming start to our new life in Gran Canaria.

As a journalist and writer, I would often spend my morning sitting in a café bar in the main street of our nearby town simply people watching. It always gave me ideas and inspiration for stories, and I was fascinated by the people who walked past my table. People of all skin colour and ethnicity passed by who were often dressed in colourful outfits and dresses, smart suits and work clothes.

Chinese, Korean, African and Europeans surrounded me, chattering in different languages to each other, as well as on their mobile phones. Drag Queens, often in various states of dress or undress, with sweaty make up dripping down their faces, often swept by on their way home from the numerous clubs and bars.

The island was always one with a strong 'live and let live attitude'; no one cared whether you were straight, gay, bisexual or simply confused. Whether you were Christian, Buddhist or Muslim didn't matter, just as long you lived your life in a way that avoided upset or hurt to others.

After our experiences as a gay couple in the UK, where spiteful, judgemental attitudes prevailed for so long, this attitude of freedom meant so much to David and myself. There were occasional petty quarrels, but overall, there was a genuine feeling of cooperation and working together for the common good.

In the various café bars that David and I visited for our morning coffee, we usually spotted a couple of local police officers enjoying their mid-morning break. Over time, we were recognised and became acquainted with many of these men and woman. They were always friendly to us and often made jokes about the British and their activities on the island. It was good natured banter, which also made us realise and understand the little effort that many British people made in assimilating into the community, learning the language and respecting local laws.

It appeared that the police officers took it all in good part, but they clearly thought that the British were a 'mad lot'. As friendly and helpful as we found most police officers in Spain, I should add that all police officers carry guns, so respect is expected and, indeed, demanded. Our usual contact was with local police officers. These men and women are appointed by the mayor of the municipality and responsible for dealing with some of the minor incidents.

I recall on one occasion, a local police officer arriving at our home on his motor bike to give us a bill for the preceding five years of council tax, which we had not paid, simply because we had never received a bill, despite several requests from ourselves. The police officer was very cheerful and was clearly enjoying his morning out and the coffee that he gratefully accepted.

The next tier of police is the Guardia Civil, who often used to be referred to unkindly as 'Franco's Thugs'. These are a paramilitary police force, usually housed in secure local barracks. They are effective, no nonsense and often harsh in their methods, but they get the job done. They are not police officers to argue with, and despite the Franco years being long over, they still command deep respect.

I recall, as a reporter, having an interview with them in a depressing room with no windows about a story I had written, and a contact who needed further investigation. It was not a pleasant interview and I recall wishing that I had taken a lawyer with me to the interview. There were times during the interview when I was made to feel like the guilty party. Fortunately, they let me leave, and thanked me for my trouble.

The third tier of Spanish police is the National Police. These are professional, highly trained and respected officers dealing with major crime. They usually share their areas with the Guardia Civil with some municipalities being the responsibly of the Guardia Civil, whilst other municipalities are the responsibility of the Policia National.

Some years ago, politicians came up with the bright idea of merging both the Policia National and the Guardia Civil. There was such an outcry from members of the Guardia Civil that the idea was quietly and quickly forgotten; they still retain considerable influence in Spain. The idea of merging the two police forces was a sensible one, but I doubt it will ever happen.

Returning to the UK to live, I often speak to neighbours and local people, and many local people are concerned about the lack of police support in the area. I sense this too, and like so many other local people feel that the responsibility rests upon ourselves to do our best to protect ourselves. South Devon is a major area for tourism that brings together many thousands of people from across the country.

Crime is an issue here, just as it is in other areas and cities with much higher permanent populations. I know that funding is an issue, but much is determined by spending priorities, and I sense that gimmicks, such as the appointment of Police and Crime Commissioners is little more than a sticking plaster attempting to cover a major problem.

I contrast the weak level of police support in the UK to that we have witnessed in Spain and the Canary Islands just a short time ago. We are sometimes asked if we feel safe here. Sadly, my answer must be no, we do not.

Orchids, Gardening and Cats

I recall homes being flooded and cars swept away during one particularly bad storm a few years ago. For the remainder of the year, it was usually dry and sunny, with temperatures sometimes reaching or exceeding 30 degrees, which was not ideal growing conditions for most plants, other than cactus.

I have always loved plants and enjoy seeing a well-maintained garden. This was one of the first things that I missed when we moved to the Costa Blanca, and even more so when we moved to the Canary Islands.

In most cases, the Spanish do not seem to have a great appreciation of gardens, although I will no doubt be corrected by examples of some spectacular botanical gardens in the country, including a superb example in the North of Gran Canaria. I am, of course, speaking of people's homes. Many Spanish people live in apartments and there is little opportunity to have a garden, other than maybe a window box or a few tubs on the patio.

Sadly, even these few examples are often badly neglected, and it is not unusual to see plants in containers that have been ignored for several weeks, so are shrivelled and dead, with no attempt to replace them until possibly the following year, or if one is given as a gift.

Garden centres in the UK are splendid affairs. Most have developed from being stockists of both indoor and outdoor plants to major suppliers of gifts, greetings cards, garden accessories and all manner of items for the home, as well as the garden. The best part of the UK garden centre is, in my opinion, the café. It would be very unusual to find one that did not offer cream teas and a delicious selection of cakes and pastries.

I contrast this to the few that I have found in Spain; at best they should be called shops selling plants rather than garden centres. If you are lucky, you might find an automatic machine dispensing water or cola, but that's about it.

When we moved to the Costa Blanca, I remember being encouraged by a neighbour and a very good friend, to install a water pipe throughout the garden before the patio was completed. It was good advice, since we could ensure that plants that were set directly into the soil, as well as plants in containers, would receive a regular supply of water controlled through an automatic timer. Plants were quickly established and provided a lush green and bright backdrop to what would have been a dry, arid garden. We did have rain in the Costa Blanca, of course, but it was spasmodic; there was always too much rain or none.

Our move to the Canary Islands was a little more traumatic when it came to the availability of plants and gardening. We moved to a dry, arid part of the island that offered little more than desert conditions throughout much of the year. In February, we usually had huge storms with very heavy downpours of rain and flooding that lasted for two or three days.

There was usually a lot of damage, which was often quickly forgotten when the sun came out for another year. I recall homes being flooded and cars swept away during one particularly bad storm a few years ago. For the remainder of the year, it was usually dry and sunny, with temperatures sometimes reaching or exceeding 30 degrees, which was not ideal growing conditions for most plants, other than cactus.

The islands are awash with cactus of all shapes and varieties. Although I quite like seeing them and admire some of the huge prickly ones adorned with flowers on many of Gran Canaria's roundabouts, we had our dogs Bella and Barney to consider.

Barney was a wise, but lazy dog, who would not consider going anywhere near a cactus, but Bella was still young and slightly crazy, and we never quite knew what she was up to. Digging large holes was her speciality, and we could easily imagine nursing a dog with very sore paws if she went anywhere near a cactus.

Our new home had a small, but functional front garden with a soil filled area, as well as a rear patio, which had some tiles and decorative stones. We decided to focus on planting the front garden but would use containers for plants in the rear garden area, which would allow the reminder of the area to be used by Barney and Bella. We installed another automatic watering system, which our neighbours thought to be very wasteful of water.

Our water supply came from the mountains, as well as from desalination; it was expensive, so we had to be careful. I reasoned that since most of our neighbours seemed to thoroughly wash their cars each week, using plenty of water, I was using about the same for our small garden. The timer was set for only a short period twice a day, which was just sufficient to stop the plants shrivelling.

The choice of plants was the next issue. After a few trial runs, I discovered that roses did remarkably well in our front garden. I was initially told that roses did not stand a chance in our dry part of the island, but since we lived just a minute or two from the sea, the humidity seemed to suit them. In addition, we never had any problems with black spot, greenfly or other issues that are often the curse of roses in the UK.

We also planted French lavender, not the British variety, since the French variety lasts for several years and have much brighter, resilient flowers and a heady perfume. Although I generally dislike geraniums and pelargoniums because of their perfume, and the sap that brings me out in a rash, I relented, since they will grow almost anywhere. We were right, and we had a splendid display of these three main plants throughout the year.

We did find two excellent garden centres, as opposed to shops that sell plants, on the island, even though they did not have a café. This is where we bought several plants that would be considered as highly specialist in the UK, but little more that cheap, ordinary plants in Spain. Plants such as frangipani (also known as plumeria) and strelitzia (bird of paradise) became highly prized specimens and soon featured in containers on our rear patio.

Indoor plants are another love of mine and I had a magnificent collection of orchids when we lived in Dorset. Sadly, our move to Spain meant that I had to find new homes for them. When we arrived in Gran Canaria, I once again caught the bug and started to buy orchids, as well as other indoor plants for our new garden room, which we had built as a new addition to the property.

The orchids did not do particularly well, until I finally came to terms with the fact that that I would have to switch from those orchids requiring a cool or moderate temperature to those that would accept much more heat.

Our gardening efforts in the Canary Islands went well, and many people used to admire our efforts and compliment us as they walked past our small front garden. There was not a lot of competition, since most Spaniards prefer to tile over or concrete any patch of bare soil that they see.

Our next-door neighbours had a few pots of long shrivelled plants, whilst others had large overgrown trees in their front garden that were in danger of causing real damage to the foundations, and walls of the property.

A few years later, when we had lost our much-loved dog, Barney, a kitten dropped into our lives. We don't know where he came from, but he had clearly fallen from top of the high walls surrounding our home. He was barely past the weaning stage, and we had no choice but to care for this tiny scrap of life. Although we both like cats, we didn't really want to adopt one, since we could not cope with one that also went outdoors and killed birds and other creatures.

Cats are generally treated very badly on the islands; they are treated as vermin and regularly poisoned. We were very aware of heart-breaking stories of cats dying cruelly in this manner and we didn't want this worry. Mac, as we called him, quickly grew into a healthy, much-loved member of our little family. Bella basically ignored him, although Mac was intrigued by her, and particularly fascinated with her tail, which Bella did not appreciate.

There was no longer any question of rehoming him, but the deal was that he would be a house cat and never allowed outdoors. As it turned out, Mac never looked to go outside anyway, and was very happy following the sunshine around the various rooms of our home.

Soon after Mac moved in, we realised that we would have to lose most of our indoor plants. This was not because Mac would jump on them and destroy them, which he would if he had the opportunity, but because most were poisonous to cats.

I did some careful research and finally gave away all our indoor plants, other than orchids that were safe for cats to eat, if they chose to. We hoped that Mac would avoid the temptation, which he usually did. As a result of Mac's tolerance, my orchid collection grew both in size and variety.

How I missed lawns and the smell of newly cut grass when we moved to the island. Bella, our little Spanish girl, only saw grass once during her fifteen years of life. She would run on the beach, play on gravel and tiled patios but only once was she able to play on grass. She was already a little elderly and was enjoying herself so much that she overdid it and had to be carried home. We were very concerned about her, and avoided doing it again, which we later regretted.

The neighbours who lived behind our home grew a very small lawn, which I can best describe as being the size of a large tablecloth. On most Sunday mornings, and if I was quick enough to catch it, our neighbour would cut the grass with a small Flymo mower. It took seconds, but the perfume was poignant and reminded me of our previous life in the UK.

Once again, during our planned return to the UK, I had to dispose of all my orchids, because we were not allowed to bring them into the country from the islands that were technically outside the European Union (although part of Spain).

David arranged this when I was away sorting out issues in the UK, thoughtfully realising that it would be upsetting to see some of my favourite orchids passed on to neighbours and friends. He also found homes for many of our container plants, which were gratefully accepted by friends and neighbours. By the time that I returned to Gran Canaria for the last time, all the orchids and both front and rear gardens were completely bare of any plant life.

It was almost as if we had never lived there, which I found deeply unsettling. Still, we have always said that "Home is where the fluffies are", and so it was time to make a success of our decision and our new home in the UK.

When we moved to our new home in South Devon, we were faced with a garden that was mostly neglected and overgrown. Sufficient had been done to ensure that plants and trees did not encroach on neighbours' property, but there were several magnificent trees and shrubs that badly needed drastic pruning. Over time, David worked hard on restoring the garden to its former glory. New plants were purchased to replace those that had to be removed, whilst retaining much of the general design of the garden.

I had by then purchased some wonderful new battery-operated garden tools, courtesy of Amazon's next day delivery, and was able to make a start on hacking back, pruning and cutting branches. It was hard, but mostly enjoyable work. Fortunately, work on restoring the garden came during the period of Covid lockdown. We were able to focus upon restoring the garden simply because there was very little else that we could do.

Sadly, garden centres were closed during that period, and it was thanks to supermarkets such as Tesco, Lidl and Morrison's that we were able to purchase plants at a relatively low price, which I assume was because nurseries could not sell their stock to garden centres.

We also bought some rather expensive, but well-established shrubs and trees from a specialist nursery in Cornwall that was happy to dispatch by courier. These were beautiful specimen plants, and it was money well spent.

So, what about orchids? Having established several collections over the years, and then having to dispose of them, I felt disheartened and not keen to repeat the process, and so I initially decided not to get involved again. It was only when my brother and family arrived to welcome us to our new home, and presented us with a beautiful phalaenopsis orchid, that I changed my mind.

As good fortune would have it, our new home in South Devon was very close to one of the largest and well-established orchid nurseries in the UK, Burnham Orchids. I remember last visiting the nursery over thirty years earlier when it was owned and run by Brian Ritterhousen and his sister, Wilma.

It was Brian and his gentle enthusiasm who first inspired me to collect these beautiful and often very unusual plants, whilst Wilma inspired me with her writing. I still have several of Wilma's books, which were ahead of their time in detail, photographs and explanations; they have been well thumbed over the years. I also recall Brian's daughter, Sara working in the nursery, as well as a young man called Arthur.

Although Brian and Wilma have passed, Sara continues the family business in running the nursery, and still ably assisted by an older Arthur. When we returned to the nursery after so many years away, it really was like coming home. Some things had, of course changed, and there is now a tearoom, but the original ethos, specialist knowledge and helpfulness are still there and expressed in much the same way as in the days of Brian and Wilma.

I am now in the process of rebuilding my orchid collection. During those dark days of Covid lockdown, and later my cancer diagnosis, I believe that my orchids helped me through some of the most difficult days, and I know that other collectors will agree with me. It is hard to feel depressed when looking at some of the most beautiful and unusual creations in the plant world. Yes, they need understanding and care, but the rewards are great for those sensitive enough to appreciate them.

In the days before Brexit, orchid enthusiasts would often order unusual orchid specimens from European countries, such as the Netherlands, Poland and Germany. Sadly, this is no longer economic or possible because of the paperwork and delays involved. Despite this, we are well supported by Burnham Orchids and a few other UK nurseries.

As well as developing my orchid collection, we spent much of the Covid related lockdown laying turf for a new lawn, cementing and pointing crazy paving, as well as restoring an ancient bird bath with a working fountain.

This work gave us a great deal of pleasure; renovating a garden is satisfying because the result of hard work is easy to see and imagine in the years to come. Developing and enjoying our new garden was one of the many reasons that we are happy to be living in the UK once again.

This Won't Hurt a Bit

After a couple of weeks in the Costa Blanca, I was already well aware of when we were being treated as 'cash cows.' Sadly, this was one of the downsides of living in an area that was very popular with new British residents.

I have always taken regular dental check-ups very seriously. I had been a patient of my NHS dentist in Dorchester for many years. I trusted him, and as most readers will know, the trusting relationship between dentist and patient is a unique one, and not one that we give up lightly.

Of course, moving to Spain would mean that this relationship would have to come to an end, although I did keep my options open by being non-committal to the dentist about our move to Spain, believing that I would return every six months for my check-ups, possibly combining it with some inspection and consultancy work at the same time. Of course, this was not to be.

David was the first to try out a dentist in the Costa Blanca, which turned out to be a particularly unpleasant experience. He needed a new filling, and made an appointment with what was advertised as a 'Swedish Dentist' a short walk from our new home in Rojales. The dentist was pleasant enough, and she was indeed Swedish. She decided that David's teeth would need a clean and polish before she attempted a filling. Sadly, the equipment was faulty, and she spent some time trying to get it to work.

Finally, the dentist declared that the reason for it not working was that there was no water supply. Never mind, she would carry on cleaning without the inconvenience of water. As most readers will be aware, the dental cleaning process is not a pleasant one at the best of times, since it involves plenty of water to accompany the scraping tool.

Usually, a dental nurse is standing by with a suction device to remove excess water, otherwise I am told that the accompanying choking effect is similar to 'water boarding' used as a means of torture, and is best avoided. In contrast, cleaning without water should be avoided, since severe damage can be done to both teeth and gums without water acting as both a coolant and lubricant. Fortunately, at this point, David had the good sense to stop the procedure and to walk out of the surgery, and never to return.

A few days later, I attended my dental appointment with the 'German Dentist' on the other side of the road. As Sweden had let us down, we felt that Germany would probably prove to be a better bet, although we had hoped to find a Spanish dentist.

The German dentist was abrupt and to the point. "I examine and I clean. I remove all those old fillings and replace all with new white ones. Maybe a crown or two as well. Yes?" The answer from me was a definite "No".

After these two unfortunate encounters, David and I decided to have our dental treatment when we were next in the UK and, in the meantime, ask around and find a Spanish dentist who we could trust.

After a couple of weeks in the Costa Blanca, I was already well aware of when we were being treated as 'cash cows.' Sadly, this was one of the downsides of living in an area that was very popular with new British residents. We were often seen as a source of easy money, and many Brits are usually far too polite to question and challenge, particularly in a new country.

We soon became aware that many British people were exploited, with few challenging what they saw as 'professional people', such as dentists, vets, estate agents and even lawyers. Later, when I began to work as a reporter for an English language newspaper, I often reported and warned about such scams. Although such practices were not always illegal, there was always a fine line between legality and sharp practice. They provided me with a steady stream of good stories, which made me popular with readers, but less so with the perpetrators of the various scams.

One of the problems was that few British residents bothered to learn Spanish and took 'special offers' and 'advice' at face value instead of doing some research. As a result, many were often at the complete mercy of unscrupulous people. There were, of course, more sinister crimes that new British residents became victims of, but are stories for another time.

Returning to the UK sixteen years later, my Dorchester dentist had long since retired, and it was time to find another dentist in our new home town of Teignmouth. Finding a dentist in the town was not an immediate priority for us, since getting our new home into a liveable condition was top of the list. We soon found an excellent veterinary surgery for Oscar and Merlin, but our search for a doctor and dentist came much later in our plans.

I thought it would be easy, but all dentists that I called claimed that they were no longer taking NHS patients. I telephoned an NHS helpline that is supposed to match patients with NHS dentists in their area, but was told that we would have to wait "about three years" before an NHS dentist could be allocated to us, and that may not be even in the same town. Three years later, and we are still waiting…

It was clear that we would have to go private, which was not really an issue, since we already had to pay for any dental treatment in Spain and the Canary Islands. Spain's NHS did not cover any dental treatment, other than in exceptional cases. That said, dental charges are much lower in Spain than in the UK, and I was horrified when the first bill for cleaning and a filling was presented; despite this, we are once again very happy with our new dental practice.

My memory goes back to my days as a headteacher of a Dorset village school, when the school dental service would arrive for a few days to check the teeth of my pupils, and occasionally staff! A caravan would be set up in the school playground, and the dentist and dental nurse would become part of the school team for a few days.

They were kind, friendly people, and I recollect only very few occasions when children either refused to be treated or became exceptionally stressed. On those very rare occasions, it was usually the over bearing or fussy parents that were the problem. We could all agree that it was one of those occasions when it was preferable that parents were nowhere to be seen.

Despite our dental issues in the Costa Blanca, we received an entirely different experience in Gran Canaria, which I believe was representative of dentistry in Spain. Most British people relocating to Spain will discover that Spanish dentistry is very good.

It is mostly private based, with no National Health Service support, and strongly supported by private medical insurance schemes. There has been considerable investment in dentistry over the years and many young people made dentistry their profession, and this led to a situation where there were too many qualified dentists in the country.

Many newly qualified dentists subsequently moved to other parts of Europe, and particularly to the UK, where they established lucrative practices, and often in areas where there was no dental surgery, and offered treatment under the UK's National Health Service, which came as a relief to many patients.

Sadly, I am told that this position has now moved into reverse, since many Spanish dentists, as well as those from other European countries, have left the UK following Brexit. As a result, there is once again a shortage of dentists to support the work of the NHS. Over time, dental care in Spain moved full circle and there became a shortage of Spanish dentists working in the country.

This gap was filled with many dentists moving from South America, where Spain has many historical, cultural and trade links, and many dentists from Argentina and Cuba, particularly, established new practices in Spain and the Canary Islands.

During our years in Spain, we discovered new treatments and specialisms offered in Spain that were often unavailable in the UK. One example of this is dental implants, which is now becoming much more common, yet only a few years ago, our dental surgery in the Canary Islands was one of a limited number that offered this specialist surgery in Spain and much of Europe.

Indeed, it is now possible to have dental implants fitted in one day, and could be part of your holiday in the Canary Islands! Indeed, as with many other medical treatments, such as breast implants and cosmetic surgery, medical tourism became part of the new tourist economy of the islands.

When David and I launched an English language newspaper in Gran Canaria, we met a highly talented and experienced dentist from Argentina, Carlos, who with his wife, Ester, had recently established a new dental practice in Gran Canaria. Carlos wanted to buy advertising in our newspaper, and asked us to write promotional features that would help him to establish his new surgery, particularly with English speaking residents.

Carlos was one of very few dentists at that time specialising in dental implant surgery, working in both Madrid, as well as the island. Over the years, we watched the surgery grow in popularity. Additional dentists and support staff soon joined the surgery, which rapidly expanded into larger premises.

By the time that we left, Carlos had established three new surgeries on the island, as well as other practices on neighbouring islands. In addition, another building housed staff and equipment to make dentures, implants and other dentistry essentials.

Naturally, Carlos and his wife became our dentists, and we took huge pleasure, and some credit, in watching the practice grow and develop so successfully over just a few years.

I am sure that one of the reasons behind the growth of dental businesses in Spain is the Spanish love of sweets. I have rarely seen such emporiums of sweets elsewhere that I saw in Spain and the Canary Islands! It certainly puts the old 'Pick and Mix' delights to shame. These sweet shops are usually full of customers, and the large bags of sweets that are carried out of these shops makes me wonder about the health of their teeth.

Most banks, lawyers, accountants, veterinary surgeries, hotels, restaurants and other businesses have a basket of boiled sweets on their counters, or in their waiting rooms, to tempt customers as they pay their bills, or carry out other business. Adults and children alike grab handfuls of these tempting offerings, sucking and chewing as they leave the establishment. I am quite sure that this is frowned upon in the UK.

When It's Gone, It's Gone

The Canarian village where we lived did not have a pier, but an impressive harbour wall that looked and felt a little like walking on a pier. It had a small lighthouse at the end, which was still used to guide boats into the small harbour.

One of the many things that I was looking forward to when returning to live in the UK was revisiting the Grand Pier in Teignmouth once again. Teignmouth Pier, or Teignmouth Grand Pier, as it is more correctly known, was built in 1867 and is one of only two remaining piers left in Devon, together with the pier in Paignton.

I remember the Grand Pier from visiting the town many years earlier. It was a small and not particularly impressive structure, but a pier, nevertheless. I also remember that it had amusements and other entertainments too. I was looking forward to seeing it once again.

The Canarian village where we lived did not have a pier, but an impressive harbour wall that looked and felt a little like walking on a pier. It had a small lighthouse at the end, which was still used to guide boats into the small harbour. This was where I often walked with Barney and Bella during their early morning walk.

It was usually very quiet, with very few people, other than fisherman around. It was still cool and fresh, since the sun had not had time to warm up the new day. Walking out to the small lighthouse, felt just like walking on a pier. I used to sit at the end of the harbour wall, next to the lighthouse, looking at a brilliant blue, cloudless sky and a slightly darker blue sea to match. It was a perfect view that I will never forget.

I think my interest in piers may have started when I was about nine years old, when I was abandoned in Skegness. I was due to participate in a Sunday school trip to Skegness. It was very exciting, because I had not been on a coach trip before. I remembered going to Skegness in the car, usually when my mother or I had a bad cold. My mother was convinced that a visit to 'bracing Skegness' was all that was needed to frighten away any lurking germs. It was a wholesome 'kill or cure remedy that always seemed to work, although I think I preferred taking medication, which was much less 'bracing'.

I think I gave my parents a letter with all the details, but I cannot be certain. The Sunday school leader told us all to bring a packed lunch for the day. I joined the coach in my home village, which was already full of faces that I recognised from Sunday School. The two Sunday School teachers sat at the front engrossed in conversation together and ignored me. I climbed on board and sat down in a seat near to a thin, wiry boy who I recognised.

He was called Walter, and he was sitting next to his mother. Walter's mother nodded and smiled; Walter and I had a stilted conversation for a short time. I quickly realised that I had very little in common with Walter, and even our short conversation was hard going. Looking around the coach, it soon dawned on me that all the other boys and girls, who I knew from Sunday school, were accompanied, mainly by their mothers, although some had their fathers present too.

The dreadful thought soon entered my mind that this was not a Sunday School trip for children, but a day out for the entire family. Something had gone badly wrong, and my parents were unaware that they should have come along too. Looking back at that experience, I recall that the two Sunday School teachers were so involved with each other on the front seat of the coach, that they were completely unaware that there was a nine-year-old on board without any accompanying adult.

There was little I could do, although I hoped that I could tag along with Walter and his mother for the day. Walter's mother seemed friendly enough, but I wasn't too sure about Walter. The journey to Skegness was a tedious one, and I was quickly bored, and started reading a comic that I had brought with me.

When we finally arrived at Skegness bus station, I looked hopefully at Walter's mother, who gave me a cursory glance and a curt "Have a good day, Barrie. No doubt we will see you on the way home," before she and Walter left the coach.

I remember feeling both tearful and sick. I wasn't too sure what I should do, as I didn't know anyone in Skegness. However, I did remember seeing the ornate clock and the pier. Maybe I should go there? I was the last one to get off the coach. The two Sunday School teachers had long disappeared, so I made my way out of the coach station, following the rest of the group as best I could.

I quickly lost them, but had the good sense to aim for the town clock and tried to remember how I got there from the coach station. I don't recall much more of the day, other than the fact I had no watch, so I had to keep returning to the clock to see the time. I remember walking on the pier and admiring the fact that I could walk out to sea without getting my feet wet. It must have been free to visit, since I had no money to pay for an entrance ticket anyway. The idea of a building built into the sea fascinated me. I have since learned that this pier was built in 1881 and is the fourth longest pier in England.

I soon ate my sandwiches, but remember feeling hungry for the rest of the day. I had no money with me either; how I longed for an ice cream. I do remember my parent's anger when I finally arrived home and my father's cross words with the two Sunday School teachers about their lack of responsibility and care of their young charges.

Since I always hated going to Sunday School, the best part of the experience was not being sent to Sunday School again. I was also given a Timex watch for my birthday, which I still have.

Another of my very fond memories of piers is that of Bournemouth Pier. Once again, there were the usual issues of funding necessary maintenance, Bournemouth Pier always seemed to be well supported. I remember seeing many performances in the small theatre on the Pier, including musicals performed by local theatre groups, as well as popular seaside entertainers, such as Hinge and Bracket.

This would usually be followed by drinks in the cosy bar during the interval and opportunities to meet and chat with 'stars' at the end of the show. I remember having hilarious conversations with Sue Pollard, Les Dawson and John Inman, to name just a few.

There was also a spacious restaurant at the end of the pier that offered spectacular views. David and I used to have Sunday lunch there just before I had to set off on my usual week's inspection to a school in England or Wales. Although lunch was always excellent, I used to dread those final few minutes when I had to say goodbye to David and head off on one of my long journeys. I would be away from home for a week and missed it dreadfully.

Bournemouth Pier started life as a wooden jetty in 1855, replaced by a wooden pier in 1861 and an iron version in 1880. Over the years, usual deterioration set into the structure, and although the pier is still council owned, private funding was sought to fund repairs and future development.

One memorable event for Bournemouth Pier was in August 1993 when the IRA threatened to blow the pier to pieces on its 50th birthday. Thankfully, the bomb did not go off, due to a malfunctioning detonator, which is just as well, since Sue Pollard, Lionel Blair and Les Dennis were performing to an audience of 800 people at the time.

The pier is now operated by a private company. Sadly, the historic pier theatre was finally closed, despite considerable public protests, and replaced with an 'adventure sports attractions' and 'zip wire'. Despite public concerns about closure of the theatre and some opposition to some of the zanier projects proposed for the pier, the local council appear to have maintained overall control of the pier, whilst allowing change of use and some imaginative developments by private companies.

It is this lack of overall council oversight and support that appears to be lacking for Teignmouth Pier. Teignmouth Pier is a big disappointment. It is badly in need of major repair and general maintenance. Part of the pier is now closed and will eventually be removed because it is dangerous. The part of the pier that is still open contains an interesting collection of elderly 'coin in the slot 'machines, which are fascinating to see and try out. I recall one that contains several 'Pelham' string puppets. These rarities are many years old, and it is fascinating to see them jig and dance when a coin is put into the slot; it is like going back in time.

Repairs to the pier are becoming urgent, I have seen several photographs showing severe rust and deterioration of the metal structures that support the wooden decking; several of the metal supports are severely bent too. The Grand Pier was sold to a private family by the local council many years ago. Despite continual pressure from the general public for "something to be done", the usual excuses of "no money", "we cannot interfere with private property", "it is not eligible for National Lottery funding" are just a few of the reasons why this much-loved local attraction will one day be destroyed in a bad storm.

Whatever happens to the Grand Pier in the future, I hope it can be rescued before it is too late. It is worrying to think that yet another Victorian era construction, which was built and funded for the public good, has stood proudly and used for so long by generations of visiting holidaymakers, now sits sad and neglected.

Why is it that the present generation cannot be bothered to value its heritage? When Teignmouth Pier finally succumbs to the inevitable, I can already imagine the howls of protest from the local community, as well as from holidaymakers who regularly visit this popular seaside town. Why not step in early and prevent this from happening?

A Nice Cup of Coffee

Life in Spain and the Canary Islands is always taken at a much more leisurely pace and eating and drinking is an event to be taken seriously; to enjoy and never to be rushed.

On most mornings, our dog Bella and I would walk the few minutes from our home in Gran Canaria to a friendly and welcoming café bar on the promenade. The cafe bar is beautifully situated at the edge of the promenade, usually overlooking a brilliant blue sea, and an accompanying blue sky.

As it was early morning, there were few people about, other than a few fishermen tending their boats and nets, and other dog walkers like myself. The café bar was very popular with locals and tourists alike. It served a range of traditional Canarian dishes at fair prices, the produce was always fresh, beautifully cooked and served.

I usually ordered an 'espresso' coffee or maybe an 'Americano'; much would depend upon whether the café bar had received their supply of fresh croissants from the village bakery. If I was in a hurry, it would be an 'espresso', if I wanted to linger with a croissant, and 'people watch' it would be an 'Americano'.

Often, I didn't even have to order, one or the other would appear almost immediately on my table. It was some of the best coffee that I have ever tasted and remained at the same price all the time that we lived there – just 90 cents.

Returning to the UK, I was expecting to see the usual manic charge of office workers and shoppers going about their morning business, clutching a mobile phone in one hand and a cigarette in the other.

How things have changed in the years that we have been away from the UK. It seems that the current trend is to purchase coffee from one of the trendy and expensive coffee shops that seem to have appeared everywhere and use the plastic or paper coffee mug as a kind of weapon as they charge to their place of work, holding their coffee at arm's length in front of them. It always amazes me why folk cannot simply have a cup of coffee before they leave home, or put the kettle on when they got to work? Why cannot they relax for a few minutes whilst they enjoy drinking it? Is modern life in the UK really that manic?

I am relieved to witness the fact that few people now drink instant coffee, which was an old favourite with many people not so long ago. It seems that the UK population is gradually being exposed to some of the finer things in life, such as decent coffee. The European influence maybe?

There is no doubt in my mind that British understanding of coffee has developed in recent years, due to the influence of Europeans, who have always understood the value of a decent cup of coffee, whilst they holiday in the sun. As for that wartime coffee lookalike, 'Camp Coffee', which seemed to find its way into the 1970's, whatever happened to that?

Thankfully, life in Spain and the Canary Islands is always taken at a much more leisurely pace and eating and drinking is an event to be taken seriously; to enjoy and never to be rushed. Even when having a simple cup of coffee before work, the Spanish will savour it, and use it as an opportunity to chat with other customers and the staff serving them. It would be a very rare sight indeed to see Spanish or Canarians charging along the street holding a cup of coffee in front of them as they make their way to work!

Depending upon when work starts, or if they have already started work, it may also be an opportunity to order a 'bocadillo '(large filled crusty roll) to keep them going until lunchtime. Neither is it unusual to see police officers sitting in cafes, enjoying their morning coffees too. I can think of no better way to get acquainted with the local community, but I have no doubt that the UK police authorities would regard this community approach as rather strange.

I am always puzzled by the large number of expensive and trendy looking coffee shops in the UK, selling equally expensive coffees and pastries. People seem to flock to these businesses in large numbers, and it is not unusual to see large queues forming in chains such as Costa Coffee, Starbucks and others.

I have tried to visit one or the other a few times, but rarely have the patience to wait for long, and often leave before I am served. Apart from the ridiculous range of coffees being offered and the endless questions of "Would you like sprinkles?", the biggest irritations for me are the horrendous noises emitted from these coffee making monsters. They are so noisy that I sometimes wonder how the staff cope with working with them all day.

Why is it I cannot simply request an 'Americano' without being asked for the size of coffee, variety and, worse still "black or white?" Do I want sprinkles or a marshmallow maybe? No, No, No! In Spain, 'Americano' is always a black coffee, and never offered with milk. As for the prices being charged, I am a long way from paying 90 cents for cup of coffee in Gran Canaria, since I last paid £3.50 for a weak, miserable alternative in 'Costa Lottee'. I now know why most people use a credit card to pay for their coffee in the UK, it is just so expensive.

Despite my criticism of these 'coffee emporiums', I am always amazed and delighted to see the huge and delicious range of cakes and pastries to accompany coffee, albeit at frightening prices. For me, this is an unusual sight, since this was not my experience in Spain and the Canary Islands. At best, most café bars would stock one variety of mass-produced donuts, or maybe a slab of something akin to what British people would see as a rather dry madeira cake, but sometimes covered in thick chocolate.

A range of delicious looking cakes and pastries would be restricted to patisseries and rarely seen in café bars. Even then, the delicious looking cakes and pastries would turn out to be very disappointing, and usually filled with tasteless, artificial cream. As someone who has always had a sweet tooth, the Spanish experience was a good one for me, health wise, since few of these disappointing pastries ever tempted me. Goodness knows how I will cope with the delicious offerings in the UK coffee shops and bakeries.

Our café bar in Gran Canaria knew how to tempt its regular customers by offering plates of churros and hot chocolate to dip them into. Churros are best described as long, thick fried dough, a little similar to donuts in texture, which are usually eaten at breakfast. It is said that they were popular with Spanish shepherds as a substitute for freshly baked food, since it was easy to make and fry in an open fire. Churros are usually dipped in bowls of steaming hot chocolate, sprinkled with cinnamon sugar. I tried these once, but never again. Churros are delicious, disgustingly fattening and best avoided if you wish to remain healthy and live a long life.

Few people know that coffee is also grown in Gran Canaria, as it has been since 1788 when King Carlos III issued a decree ordering the introduction of the first coffee plants to the Island. Today, coffee is produced in very small amounts by local farmers who have kept the tradition of growing and consuming the coffee that they produce for many generations. This very special coffee is called Finca la Corcovada and is grown in the Valley of Agaete.

This valley has a microclimate and a rich soil and is perfect for growing coffee. The coffee is grown and produced by Juan Godoy, the only coffee grower in Europe and who is now supplying the UK market. I tried a sample once, and it is delicious. My aim is now to try and purchase a regular supply in the UK, which will add a taste of Canarian sunshine to my cup of morning coffee.

Empty Shelves and Empty Pumps

There is the plus side; there is nothing that a home-grown Brit likes more than a good crisis, after all it "Brings out the Dunkirk Spirit" screams one of the tabloids. I'm not sure about that assessment, but it does allow for a good moan, which the British have always been rather good at.

At the time of writing, the UK is in the grip of an acute shortage of lorry and tanker drivers. Many shoppers are reporting empty supermarket shelves, there are queues at petrol stations due to a shortage of tanker drivers, gas and electricity prices are rocketing due to gas shortages, utility companies are going bust and to crown it all, it looks as if there will be no turkeys for Christmas, and it is only mid-September.

In addition, there is widespread concern about what is seen by many as the collapse of the National Health Service, with warnings that it could take up to ten years to clear the cancer treatment backlog that has accrued during the pandemic. Despite current problems, there is reluctance, indeed resistance, in the British media to accept that many of the issues are due to Brexit.

Many people, and indeed ourselves, have friends and colleagues in Europe, and they are not reporting any shortages of food on supermarket shelves, shortages of lorry drivers, queues at petrol stations or breakdown in their health services.

The right-wing tabloids, and indeed the BBC, continually blame "the pandemic", for the current situation, whilst many thinking people are fully aware that it is not purely the pandemic, but Brexit that is the problem. Of course, there is the plus side; there is nothing that a home-grown Brit likes more than a good crisis, after all it "Brings out the Dunkirk Spirit" screams one of the tabloids.

I'm not sure about that assessment, but it does allow for a good moan, which the British have always been rather good at. Besides, it's never 'our fault', even though we voted for this mess, is it?

"The problem is that no one wants to work nowadays," came the comment from one of our neighbours. "All they want are benefits and furlough money, which they don't have to work for. They should be forced to work if they take the money," Lorna grumbled, staring at me crossly with her brown, accusing eyes.

I think that Lorna already suspected that I am very much left of centre politically, whilst she is very right of centre, which I quickly deduced from the number of times that I had seen her carrying a Daily Mail lovingly in her arm whenever I passed her in town. Knowing that this could potentially be a long and arduous conversation, I smiled, nodded and tried to move on.

"It's all those foreigners that have been taking our jobs for years. Now they've gone, our people don't know how to do the jobs. It's all happened so quickly. Don't get me wrong, I'm pleased they've gone, but it's a real disgrace, that's what it is. Don't you agree?"

With an offer like that, how could I possibly refuse? I had the time, and rather fancied a decent conversation from another point of view. Anyway, I liked Lorna, so I would hate to disappoint.

"It's not quite like that, Lorna. I take your point, but the Brits never wanted to do these jobs in the first place. When I was growing up in Lincolnshire, getting workers to work on the fields was always a problem. Lincolnshire is often called the garden of England, because of all the cabbages, cauliflowers and fruit it produces. There are canning factories, abattoirs, food processing plants and all manner of businesses dedicated to food. As a teenager, I helped to pick broad beans and peas for a local farmer during the holidays with many other schoolchildren, simply because no one else wanted to do it and the farmers were desperate."

"What's that got to do with it?" asked Lorna, looking puzzled.

"My memory of rural Lincolnshire that I grew up in is of the smell of rotting vegetables and fruit. I still remember walking past endless fields of cabbages, brussel sprouts and fruit in orchards rotting away, simply because no one could be bothered to pick it. No one wanted the work then either, it was low paid, unpleasant work. That is until we joined the European Union."

"I knew you were going to bring that up. I know you think that Europe can do no wrong, but it's time we stood on our own two feet," sniffed Lorna.

"Maybe, but when we joined Europe, many workers from Poland, Romania and other countries came during the picking season to work. Later, workers from other countries came, simply because wages were higher in England than in those countries. They had the opportunity to earn what seemed to them a lot of money for their families.

"Why didn't they go home afterwards then?" asked Lorna angrily.

Most did go back at the end of the picking season; others stayed and brought their families to the UK. The farmers were happy, as they had reliable people working cheaply for them. All they had to do was to provide them with very basic accommodation. Everyone was happy."

"Except us. Look what happened then! We were overrun with them!" Lorna retorted angrily.

I battled on, ignoring the last comment. "Lorry drivers came too. They brought a wide range of goods from Europe for us to enjoy including fruit and vegetables from France, Spain and warmer countries that we couldn't get in the UK. We soon found that we had enough lorry drivers, we didn't have food shortages and petrol stations that couldn't get fuel due to a lack of drivers."

"That's my point," exclaimed Lorna triumphantly. "They've gone now, and we should be doing the work and not relying on foreigners."

"Brits still don't want the work, Lorna. Nothing has changed in the mindset. This is why we have the problem with food rotting in the fields again, food processing plants closed and a shortage of food in the supermarkets. It doesn't have to be black and white, does it? We need to allow European drivers and workers to continue working in the UK. We need to pay them properly too, so that they do not undercut the wages of British workers. Surely you can see that we are in a world where we all ultimately rely upon each other? This is one of the reasons why the UK was so prosperous during our years in the European Union."

Lorna grunted and decided that she should go to prepare lunch. I was left wondering why I had even bothered.

We rarely came across this anti-immigrant attitude in Spain and the Canary Islands. Immigrants were mostly welcomed on the basis that they would contribute to the prosperity of the country.

As a large, diverse country, post-Franco Spain was in desperate need of high-quality labour, and it welcomed workers from Morocco and sub-Saharan Africa to help with the task of building the country into the prosperous state that we see today.

Many immigrants were also highly skilled workers, looking for a better life in what they saw was a growing, prosperous country ready to welcome them. During Spain's incredible development of its tourist industry and the 'building boom' that was such an important factor, most building sites employed foreign workers.

Newly built hotels and restaurants saw a massive increase in non-Spanish staff anxious to work and send money to families back home. It was not only the construction, catering and hotel industries that benefitted from foreign workers; professional staff, such as lawyers, dentists, accountants and others flooded into the country too.

One of my happiest memories, which I have mentioned before, was as a reporter sitting in a café bar in our nearest large town watching the world go by. The streets would be full of people of different colour, speaking in a variety of languages, dressed in colourful clothes that expressed their culture and faith. There was rarely any trouble, and any arguments that did break out were quickly dealt with by ever present police officers, who seemed to understand their role that it was cooperation and not confrontation that won the day.

Sadly, my conversation with Lorna confirmed once again that despite the UK boasting that it is a 'multi-cultural country' and all the recent talk about "Global Britain", there remains an undercurrent of racism and jingoism amongst its people.

Looking back, I see little real change in attitudes over the last twenty years, except it is now probably less acceptable to express such views in public. I would love Lorna to see and witness the welcome and warmth expressed to foreigners in Spain and the Canary Islands, but I doubt that she would ever understand.

The Parish Sweeper

Both men worked in our part of the village for six days a week, using dried branches of palm tree as their brushes; these crude brushes were surprisingly effective at brushing up dust, litter and other debris from the village paths.

A few days after returning to the UK, I noticed a small, white van pass by. Emblazoned on the side of the van were the words 'Parish Sweeper'. I had not heard this term used before in the UK and I was intrigued to find out more.

My thoughts returned to the village in Gran Canaria that we had just left. Yes, we had 'parish sweepers' there too, but they were not called as such. I would meet two of the workers each morning as I walked Bella along the promenade. They always greeted me cheerily, and I would often stop to have a few words with them. I think they were amused by my pronunciation of Spanish and the words and tenses that I often got badly wrong, but they seemed to appreciate the effort.

Both men worked in our part of the village for six days a week, using dried branches of palm tree as their brushes; these crude brushes were surprisingly effective at brushing up dust, litter and other debris from the village paths. They pushed a smart, yellow trolley that collected the waste until it could be emptied into one of the village skips. These true 'parish sweepers' are a common sight throughout the Canary Islands and Spain, where public hygiene is seen as important for the public good.

Our village pavements were always beautifully maintained. In addition to the sweepers, a large cleansing lorry with rotating brushes would trundle down each street every week to brush and clean the roadways.

Twice a year, we received notices to clear the streets of all cars, which we would have been foolish to ignore. A huge lorry, with an accompanying tanker of water, would slowly make its way down each street, washing the road, as well as jet washing each drain. This had both advantages and disadvantages, since upon returning to our homes there would be a very strong sewage smell caused by 'blowback' from the drains. Despite this, we knew that when the rains came, which they usually did in February, the drains would be clear and able to cope with the huge quantities of water that fell over three days or so.

Looking back, I am amazed at the care and attention given to the cleaning of public spaces in Gran Canaria and how little it cost residents. Currently, we pay more each month in council tax in Devon than I paid the Canarian municipality for the entire year, and the range of public services then were far more comprehensive than we receive in Devon.

Dog poo was, until very recently, a major problem in Spain. Too many people let their dogs run without a lead on public paths and roads and failed to clean up after them. Tragically, accidents with dogs being killed or badly hurt in road accidents were all too frequent occurrences.

Over the years that we lived in Spain and the Canary Islands; we could see the culture gradually changing. Much was due to education, and it is thanks to the influence of many British and other European citizens that settled in the country that brought about many welcome and long overdue changes to animal welfare.

During our first few years in the country, it was unusual to see dogs on leads, as well as people cleaning up after their dogs. It was very difficult, if not impossible, to purchase dog poo bags, and we had to resort to using small food bags to do the job, which were not ideal. We used to buy a large stock of poo bags whenever we returned to the UK, and would ask visitors to bring some for us, along with stocks of Marmite, of course!

Over time, local laws were introduced, which threatened large fines for dog fouling. In large towns and cities, people with dogs were also asked to spray the area after their dog had urinated with water. This became a common sight in cities and towns, although sadly not in our village where such intrusions by officials were greeted with distain, and generally ignored.

I return to the 'Parish Sweeper'; sadly, I have only seen this van twice in the three years that I have lived in Teignmouth. I am told that he (or she) empties the dog poo bins, as well as a range of other local duties, but I have never seen any actual 'sweeping' going on.

Neither am I too clear whether there is one such person and van covering the entire area or several. Whatever the situation, the 'Parish Sweeper' is well hidden from view and remains something of a mystery; it is a very evocative title though.

Our pathways are rarely, if ever, cleaned and are often covered in dog excreta, leaves and other debris. Most of the road drains are blocked, and I am told that if a drain is directly outside a property and it becomes troublesome, it is only then that the blockage is reported directly to the local council by the occupant that the drain will be cleared.

As a result, flooding is a regular occurrence in the town, but some of which could be avoided by regularly cleaning and unblocking drains. When the issue is raised, as it is regularly in social media, the council response is, of course, 'lack of funds', pointing out a huge deficit in their budget.

I find it troubling that the explanation is meekly accepted by the general public, and nothing is ever done to address the problem. As much of the issue is due to politics, I am also surprised that the same people, with similar political allegiances, are re-elected time after time; as a result, little ever changes.

One of the many delights of living in Devon is the beautiful scenery. It has been many years of living in desert-like conditions that now make me fully appreciate trees, grass, hedges and the general 'greenness' of the country.

We rarely saw grass in Gran Canaria and, although there were some beautiful forests in the north of the island, they lacked the beautiful variety of species that we see in Devon. One of the downsides of trees, hedges and grass, of course, is that they need to be maintained. Sadly, this is rarely the case in South Devon and many hedgerows, trees and shrubs in public areas are badly overgrown and rarely given the attention that they deserve.

Leaf fall, particularly in the autumn, is a considerable problem and paths are rarely, if ever swept. Leaves are left to blow to the point of least resistance, where they rot and become a haven of soft bedding for rats and other creatures to congregate and breed.

National attempts to create areas of grassland that are left undisturbed to allow plants to repopulate and form nature reserves for insects and other creatures have been welcomed and taken literally by many local councils.

This has been music to their ears, and many grassed areas are now left uncut and unattended for many months; I am sure that this is not what the environmentalists intended, but I guess it does save money, which always seems to be the priority here. Sadly, when the grass is eventually cut, another problem is created.

Instead of collecting the grass in the usual manner, strong petrol blowers are used to blow away grass cuttings, leaves and other debris from the paths. The result is a tidy path, but little thought is given to where the debris goes, which is invariably into nearby drains, creating yet more blockages, and resulting in flooding when it rains.

In Gran Canaria, the care of trees in the village is taken very seriously. As there is little rainfall, all trees have is their own automatic irrigation system. As a result, the few trees in our village did rather well and particularly a group of trees that ran the entire length of the main street.

These trees had been established for many years and had grown to a splendid size that added variety to a street that had very little to offer, other than a few shops and a laundry. Several years ago, I remember being horrified by group of municipal workers who suddenly appeared with chain saws and removed the tops off all the trees. Emotions in the village ran very high and questions were asked as to why this was done and upon whose authority.

A public meeting was called, there were many cross words spoken, but we were assured that the municipal gardeners knew what they were doing and that all would be well.

The following year, the trees that lined our street looked truly awful. They were surely dead and would have to be replaced. However, by the end of the year, we noticed that small shoots were beginning to appear and the 'locals who knew' nodded approvingly. We need not have worried, because by the time that we had left the island, the trees looked magnificent once again. They had been carefully trimmed, shaped and pruned each year following their big cut, and now looked better than at any time I remember. Yes, the municipal gardeners did know what they were doing after all.

When I say nothing is done to clean and maintain the streets in Teignmouth, some of the locals have taken the matter into their own hands. Our neighbour, for example, has gathered a group of like-minded ladies who regularly brush and clear away weeds and other debris from the street where we live.

David and I weed and attempt to maintain the public footpath adjacent to our property, whilst another neighbour repairs, and cements cracks in the crumbling pathway that has not seen any council attention for many years; I doubt that they are even aware that it exists.

Whenever the local council is blamed for its failings in providing appropriate public services, it will blame the government for "reduced funding" and their large budget deficit. It surprises, and sometimes angers me, that local representatives in South Devon simply accept the situation, as do most of the general public.

I contrast this to our life in a village in Gran Canaria where, if the municipality was failing, a public meeting would be called, there would be many angry words, and local officials would be required to explain and held to account. Without doubt, local democracy in Spain and the Canary Islands is far more effective than what I have seen in the UK at representing the general public that it is supposed to serve.

Superfast Internet Connection

We lived in a remote part of the island, and mobile phone signals from all the telecoms companies became progressively weaker as soon as we left the main town to return to our village. It was not unusual to see neighbours lurking at the end of their roads, angrily shouting into their mobile phone in a desperate attempt to allow the person at the other end to hear what they were saying.

One of the many things that we quickly learned upon returning to the UK was the continued heavy reliance upon Victorian infrastructure. The Victorians left a fine legacy of bridges, buildings, railways and, dare I mention, piers? Sadly, in recent decades very little has been done to upgrade and modernise much of this valuable legacy, and successive governments over the years have focussed too little on replacing, repairing and modernising drains, water and sewage pipes, roads and railways that are essential to present day living.

Although the Victorians did not invent the Internet, they did invent the telephone, through the efforts of Alexander Graham Bell, although attributing the true inventor to a particular invention is often open to dispute. Surprisingly, much of the country still relies upon overhead copper wires to connect our telephones, as well as the Internet.

As a result, connections are slow and often unreliable and unsuited to carry signals to the many computers and gadgets that we have in our homes and businesses. Progress has been very slow in the UK and there are still many homes in the UK that do not have reliable access to a satisfactory Internet connection.

During our early days living in the Canary Islands, the speed of Internet connection was painfully slow. As we were launching a new English-speaking newspaper for the Canary Islands, a reliable and reasonably fast Internet connection was critical to its success, particularly as the paper was put together with photos and design features added, from our parent company's office in Benidorm.

The completed newspaper would then be sent back to us by email for checking and modification before it was emailed by us to the printers who were based on the island. This process was painfully slow and troubling and resulted in many sleepless nights.

As well as a traditional telephone connection, we resorted to using dongles, mobile phones and anything that would give reliable access to the Internet. We lived in a remote part of the island, and mobile phone signals from all the telecoms companies became progressively weaker as soon as we left the main town to return to our village.

It was not unusual to see neighbours lurking at the end of their roads, angrily shouting into their mobile phone in a desperate attempt to allow the person at the other end to hear what they were saying.

For David and myself, it all came to a head during one particularly bad February storm. Thunder, lightning, heavy rain and gale force winds soon knocked out our electricity supply and the telephone connection, complete with Internet broadband connection.

A good Internet connection is one of the essentials of life and vital for maintaining links with family and friends in other parts of the world via Skype, email and for the multiplicity of online tasks that many of us take for granted nowadays.

It was even more critical for us, as we had to send copy to the newspaper's head office in Benidorm, as well as submissions of articles to several magazines. Deadlines were often very tight, and editors were usually less than forgiving when it came to delays.

There was no Internet and no electricity, and I had an urgent email to send to meet a deadline for one of my magazines. I thought that a journey to the nearest commercial centre would be a good idea; after all they offer free Wi-Fi access. It was a difficult journey across flooded roads, which proved to be of no use, since their Internet connection was not working either.

I tried several cafe bars in the town, as well as lurking outside a house of ill repute, which did have the virtue of having an open Internet connection 24 hours a day - no doubt to meet the needs of their clients! By now I was desperate for a connection - whatever the source. Sadly, Donna's House of Sinful Pleasures was not connected either!

Finally, I had an idea! I remembered that I had once managed to achieve a respectable signal outside the local mortuary. I took my laptop computer, the appropriate dongle (a clever thing that works a bit like a mobile phone to send and receive data signals) and headed off in the rain, wind and dark to the forbidding building outside the village - not a place to be on a wet, dark and stormy night.

Once in the car park I managed to climb onto a boulder and strap the dongle to a nearby post and link it with a long cable to the laptop computer in the car. After a few anxious moments, the modem burst into life, the blue light flashed, and I was at last able to send my contribution to the magazine in time to meet the deadline.

It was a short time before the reliability of connections improved. The speed was faster and there were fewer 'dropouts' to trouble us. The Canarian Government also announced that full fibre broadband would soon be installed across all the islands, and connections to Africa and Europe would be enhanced with additional cabling across the seabed.

It was a promise that was met with considerable enthusiasm on the islands by business and home users alike. We were more doubtful, since we had heard such promises many times before, and few announcements ever progressed further than the initial press conference. How wrong we were! Within a year or two of the public announcements, we could see roads being dug up, thick cables laid and all manner of metal cabinets appearing on roadsides.

Teams of technicians and other workers arrived from the Peninsular, and it was clear that installing superfast Internet was a priority for the islands. It was a sensible decision, since the Canary Islands were working hard to become a 'hub' for growing businesses working as far apart as the USA, Europe and Africa.

It was not long before teams of workers appeared in our street, mechanically digging a deep channel at one side of the road. Later, we received information from Spain's telephone company, Telefonica, that fibre optic cables would soon be installed in homes that wished to take advantage of the new service.

It would require a new modem and, most importantly, the new fibre cables would be fitted directly into the modem and not through copper cables, which was current practice in the UK, and was the main reason for such slow speeds.

The result of this expensive and surprisingly efficient, but welcome, development was that when our connection was installed, we received the blistering superfast Internet speed of 600Mbs, which contrasted to the 3-5Mbs that we had when we first moved to Spain. We were even offered 900Mbs before we left the island. This new superfast speed worked both ways, meaning that we could now send and receive draft copies of the newspaper both reliably and fast; it was a wonderful development.

One of my first tasks when we moved into our new home in Devon was to arrange for the telephone to be reconnected and to purchase an Internet package. I was intrigued to read advertisements from several suppliers promising "Superfast Broadband".

Although this was no longer necessary now that we were not involved with the newspaper, we would appreciate a fast connection for other publishing work that we are involved in. I had my doubts that it would be quite as fast as the Spanish offering, since connections to the internal modem would still be made through the original, copper cables.

Worst still, instead of the cabling being underground, which is the case in the Canary Islands, telephone connections to our new home were through an elderly overhead cable. The poles and cables that fed a telephone line into our property were in another road and were covered with ivy and other vegetation. The possibility of a fast Internet connection did not look good.

After a little research, I discovered a reliable Internet provider offering a package at a fair price and opted for their 'Superfast Broadband'. Unsurprisingly, the best that they could offer was 53 to 73 Mbs, which is presumably on a good day when the sun is shining.

They also offered a guaranteed 45 Mbs. I was thankful that we were no longer publishing the newspaper, since a drop from 600Mbs to 45Mbs would have created many problems for us. I do wonder how local businesses, and those that work from home, that rely on a fast Internet connection cope in such circumstances?

In recent months, no doubt in response to the governments promise to ensure that all properties in the UK would eventually have a workable Internet connection, we have seen many telecoms vans in the town, busily digging holes and installing new cabling. Indeed, at the time of writing, we have just had "full fibre internet connection" installed in our home. Surprisingly, the new fibre cable goes directly into the modem, and there is no longer any copper wiring in sight!

This will make quite a difference to us, since we have had many problems with the previous installation, no doubt due to the old copper wire connection being at least fifty years old. I still find it hard to get used to masses of overhead power and Internet cables in the area, some hanging limply on rotting telegraph poles.

Similar installations were mostly placed underground in Gran Canaria, although it is hard to see how this could be achieved in the UK, given the high density of built-up areas. Now let us see if the same priority will be given to the nation's badly disintegrating water and sewage pipes, as well as other key infrastructure. I wonder what the Victorians would have made of it all?

The National Health Service

We are often told by the politicians in power that the NHS is "the best in the world". This is mere convenient, political propaganda, because it isn't "the best in the world".

I have always been a supporter of the UK's National Health Service. It is something that I, like many others, have always taken for granted. Some say that the UK's NHS is rather like a state religion; you dabble with it at your peril, as the current UK Conservative Government is rapidly finding out.

My parents were involved in the early establishment of the NHS, with my father being the administrator of a newly established hospital, as well as superintendent of a children's home. My mother was matron of both the hospital and the children's home until my brother was born.

I lived and grew up in a house in the grounds of the hospital and this was very much my 'playground'. I still remember chasing through one of the two main hospital wards in the haste to reach my father's office and being gently reprimanded by the kindly, but the outwardly stern Matron Frank, if she caught me. In those days, nurses looked like nurses and matrons looked like matrons in their formidable blue uniforms, starched white aprons and impressive headgear. I was always impressed to see those little watches dangling from their uniforms and often wondered how I could get hold of one for my school uniform.

Looking back, the vision in my mind is very similar to the 'Carry on Matron' film and, for me, a convincing matron will always look like Hattie Jacques.

We are often told by the politicians in power that the NHS is "the best in the world". This is mere convenient, political propaganda, because it isn't "the best in the world". Data from many reputable organisations show that outcomes for cancer, cardiovascular disease and a range of other conditions are far better in many European countries than in the UK, which is often very low or bottom of league tables.

Where the UK does lead is that the NHS provides more for the less money invested than most other European countries. Basically, the UK is good at providing healthcare on the cheap, and relying upon the goodwill of its workers. Our experience of the Spanish Health service put the UK's NHS into perspective.

One of the many things that we had to consider when moving to Spain was our entitlement to healthcare. This was a very important issue, particularly because of David's health at the time, but we both also needed the reassurance that healthcare would be there if we needed it.

We were assured that since the UK was now a full member of the European Union, we would continue to receive healthcare in Spain free of charge under reciprocal agreements with the UK. As a backup, we were advised to also purchase a private health insurance policy, just in case, and to cover us until we became full residents of Spain, a process that would take several months.

I already had such a policy as I had been 'encouraged' to sign up to by my rather aggressive supervisor (who was an agent for the company) when I briefly worked as a civil servant many years earlier, despite my opposition to a privatised health service.

Our first experience of Spain's Health Service was not a good one. I have always had issues with my eyes that require regular monitoring. After a short time in Spain, I contacted our local doctor who made an appointment with a hospital consultant in a Costa Blanca hospital.

Although my Spanish was poor, David's was rather good as he had been having lessons. I took with me a detailed description of my condition, which my UK consultant had helpfully provided, translated into Spanish, and had learned many of the words and phrases that I thought I would need; I felt well prepared.

When we entered the consulting room, we were not invited to sit, but after our brief introduction in Spanish, the consultant made it clear that she would not see me until I returned at another time with an official medical interpreter. She was an angry woman, clearly overworked, and would not even look at my notes. We left the hospital, both annoyed and dejected.

Although at that time, my oral Spanish was poor, my written Spanish had been coming along nicely. I wrote a letter of complaint to the hospital, pointing out EU law, discrimination and a range of other issues that I thought worthy of mention. Although I fully expected my letter of complaint to be ignored, I was pleasantly surprised to receive a letter of apology a few weeks later. The letter referred to hospital pressures and confirmed that I was fully entitled to a consultation and treatment, if required. I was also offered an appointment with another consultant.

I declined the offer, since I had already returned briefly to the UK for a check-up with my regular consultant, and a further appointment was not required until later in the year. After these initial negative issues, we became quickly impressed with the Spanish Health Service and the high quality of patient care that it provided. Occasionally, we visited friends or neighbours in the local hospital, and they always told us how well they had been looked after.

At that time there was a myth that although hospital care was very good, it was Spanish tradition for families to look after family members when they were in hospital, such as providing food, laundry and washing. We saw none of this when visiting friends, with food, laundry and washing provided by hospital staff in the same way as in the UK. This is not to say that Spanish families were not involved, they were, and I suspect far more than in the UK. If they wished to provide additional care such as washing, greater food choices and treats, they did, but it was not expected.

We were always impressed with the cleanliness of Spanish hospitals. On one occasion, shortly after visiting a friend in a Spanish hospital we arrived at the same time as the cleaner. She was meticulous in moving the bed, complete with patient, mopping, dusting and wiping. Our friend told us that this was a usual and daily routine.

Sadly, this positive experience was in immediate contrast to a visit to see David's mother, who had been very poorly, and was in a Devon hospital. When we arrived to see her, she could not be found in any ward. This was alarming, and we immediately began to fear the worst. After some time, the receptionist finally found her. She had been moved into another ward, but somehow this move had not been recorded. During our long walk to the new ward, we noticed piles of unopened cardboard boxes stacked high in corridors, and in some of the smaller consulting rooms adjacent to the corridor.

We also noticed impressive layers of dust on top of the boxes, as well as on the floor. We both commented that the cleaning staff of the Spanish hospitals would have been horrified. Shortly afterwards, MRSA, which is bacteria that is resistant to most antibiotics, became a considerable issue in UK hospitals. An alarmed government, led by Prime Minister Gordon Brown, immediately ordered a "deep clean" of all hospitals; we could see why.

Our experiences of the Spanish Health Service became even more impressive when we moved to Gran Canaria. Although there was considerable initial paperwork and registration to be completed, we were eventually allocated to a doctor at our village surgery.

Our GP, Dr Herlinda, was a magnificent find, and on the rare occasions that we had cause to see her, she was always courteous, helpful and very efficient. At a time when patients in the UK were experiencing delays of up to three weeks to see a GP, we were always able to make an appointment to see her the following day by making an appointment online.

We would always be very well prepared for the consultation, making notes in Spanish for Dr Herlinda, and learning any key words that would assist our explanations. In return, Dr Herlinda, who didn't speak English, would listen patiently, and often type difficult explanations into Google Translate to help us to understand her diagnosis and treatment.

Apart from the usual anxiety experienced when visiting any doctor, a lengthy wait in the waiting room was usually to be expected and was always very entertaining. It was nearly always full of colourful and loud locals who were using their visit as a kind of community get together.

There was always talking and much laughter, despite several signs telling patients to be quiet whilst waiting. Sitting listening to the chatter that surrounded me always reminded me of the wonderful, heady contrast between the mostly gregarious Spanish and the more reserved British, who would not dream of sharing their condition and treatment with the rest of the waiting room.

From time to time, Dr Herlinda, or her colleague, Dr Elena, would appear with a list. They would then call out the names of the next six patients who were to follow in turn. Dr Herlinda would always make a point of turning to David and myself especially when our names were called, to ensure that we had heard and knew our place in the queue. There was usually a long wait. This was not because the doctors were inefficient, which they certainly were not, but they appeared not to be too constrained by time.

One of my more poignant memories was when our neighbour and good friend, Colin, became seriously ill with terminal cancer. Sometimes he was in considerable pain, or depressed and simply wanted a chat.

Dr Elena told him that he could call in to see her, without an appointment, whenever he felt the need, which he did on several occasions. I am sure that this offer was made to other patients in similar desperate and depressing circumstances and was one of the reasons for the lengthy delays in appointment times.

It was this generous patient care that was a feature of this wonderful surgery, which we were so grateful for and will never forget. As I mentioned earlier, my eyesight was a continual source of concern, and I was advised that I needed a series of operations to maintain my sight. Although impressed with the advice that we had been given by specialists in Gran Canaria, we decide that it would be sensible to get a second opinion from the experts at the world-renowned Moorfields Eye Hospital in London.

Sadly, my consultation and impression of the hospital were disappointing. The consultant agreed with the diagnosis that I had been given in Gran Canaria, which required several procedures. However, they could only resolve some of the issues, which would basically mean a reduction in my overall quality of sight. In any case, monitoring the procedures and aftercare would require a six month stay in London, which would be impossible, given our work and responsibilities on the island.

I returned very disappointed and depressed to Gran Canaria. We visited our consultant who suggested that we visit a private clinic in Las Palmas. Although I was reluctant to move from the Spanish Health Service to a private provider, I was already aware that the distinction between both sectors was much more blurred than in the UK and less divisive.

The visit to a private clinic proved to be exactly what I had been looking for. After a series of examinations, the consultant offered to operate on one eye the following week, and if all went well would operate on the second eye two weeks later. The operations were very expensive, but fortunately, my private health insurance company said that they would cover most of the expenses.

I went ahead with the procedures, and I am delighted to say that they were successful. It was only later when I was told by a consultant on the Peninsular that Gran Canaria is a specialist centre for eye and brain surgery. This was where the more difficult cases in Spain are sent for treatment. How fortunate we were to have found ourselves on an island offering such specialist treatment.

Interestingly, although the drug that I needed to take regularly was expensive and issued on a prescription from a private hospital, Dr Herlinda agreed to provide it at a much-reduced cost through the Spanish Health service, which was something that would only rarely happen in the UK.

Despite the superb care that we received at community level on the island, there were weaknesses in the healthcare system at end-of-life stage. There was little or no home-based care for patients available that we were aware of, and it was assumed that patients' relatives would step in to provide any care that was needed. This may have been appropriate for those with families, but difficult for those without anyone close to look after them, which was often the case for foreign nationals living in the country.

There were no hospices on the island either, which would have eased many of the pressures and provide help and comfort for those reaching the end of their lives. End of life care was usually provided in the last stages at the main hospitals, which was not ideal.

When we returned to the UK, we were apprehensive about the care that we would receive in Devon. We were continually hearing horror stories from friends and relatives about problems in seeing a GP and delays in subsequent treatment. It seemed to be such a contrast with the Canary Islands. However, we need not have worried. Once we had re-registered as patients in the UK, our local surgery arranged for us to have an initial examination.

In many ways, the Covid 19 pandemic has been helpful in reassessing how we go about things that we usually took for granted. In the case of our local surgery, telephone consultations quickly became the norm, with face-to-face consultations offered, if necessary.

There are now very few people spreading bugs in waiting rooms, patients are all wearing masks, and doctors seem less pressurised with time constraints. Although not everyone approves of the telephone consultation system, we much prefer it. Hospitals remain under constant pressure, which will no doubt continue until cases of Covid 19 reduce, and increased funding and staffing levels improve.

Politically, we continue to hear from our government that the UK is "world beating" in a plethora of areas, including the National Health Service. Of course, most thinking people realise that this is mostly blustering, political fluff designed to take the public's attention away from food and fuel shortages, rising energy costs, a serious shortage of nurses, as well as a chronic shortage of European 'au pairs' for the Mayfair elite.

This foolish statement is rather like comparing apples and pears, a pointless exercise. As well as the positive experience that we had with the Spanish Health service, I hear similar positive comments from British immigrants, friends and colleagues in France, Belgium and Germany.

The UK government should be aware that a successful health service depends upon the level of investment that a country makes, the range of services it provides, staffing levels together with the quality and success of its outcomes. It is time to listen and learn, and not to boast and bluster with foolish, unsubstantiated "world beating" claims.

It's Not a Proper Barbecue Unless It's Burnt

It was such a relief to discover that we were no longer being criticised and judged. Most of our new neighbours were either gay, lesbian, had gay children, were clearly gay friendly or simply didn't care.

"Come over and join our barbecue, lads" came the cheery invitation from over the wall.

This kind invitation came from one of our new neighbours, John, a retired police officer, and his South American wife, Dolores. We had only been in our new home for a few days, but had already been made welcome by many of our new neighbours.

It was such a refreshing change to find that, as a gay couple, we were being welcomed and invited to spend time with non-judgemental people who we knew would soon become our friends. It was such a relief to discover that we were no longer being criticised and judged. Most of our new neighbours were either gay, lesbian, had gay children, were clearly gay friendly or simply didn't care.

This non-judgemental attitude had hardly ever happened to us, and other gay friends, in the UK, which was one of the reasons that we left the country.

It was also ironic that our previously unnamed street had recently been given a name 'Calle San Gabriel', with Saint Gabriel apparently being adopted as the patron saint of gay men and women. Such blissful irony!

We looked over the low wall, and thanked John for his kind offer. He was cooking some kind of flesh on an open barbecue. It smelt and looked disgusting, and as vegetarians we really didn't wish to be anywhere near it.

"We can't come over right now, but how about we join you a little later?" I replied, my eyes fixed on the chunk of burnt flesh that John was poking.

"That's fine lads, we'll be here for most of the evening. We never go to bed until early morning anyway. A few more neighbours are coming over too, so it would be good for you to meet them."

"We will look forward to it. See you later."

John saw me looking and wincing at the chunk of burnt flesh. He grinned, "I always say, it's not a proper barbecue unless its burnt. Dolores loves it like this, don't you, my love?"

Dolores smiled, looked heavenwards and sighed.

What is it about so called 'real men' and their barbecues? I have often wondered about this strange phenomenon that drives some men to inflict their burnt offerings on unsuspecting visitors and friends.

It is very similar in Teignmouth where, on the very occasional days when there is no rain, the barbecues are dusted down, and we are all treated to the heady smell of charcoal and burnt flesh for most of the evening. It is something to do with the primeval instinct of 'hunter gather', I am told, but I remain unconvinced.

Barbecues are one thing, but wilfully and regularly burning garden rubbish on a bonfire on those rare days when we can hang the washing on an outside line is quite another. Black smoke headed straight towards our washing line and newly washed clothes, which we had to wash again. Our home smelt of burning for several hours, despite closing all windows. This was one of my first introductions to neighbours at our new home.

As we had returned to the country after many years away, I wanted to make sure of my facts. I did some homework and discovered that polluting activities such as this were banned in the UK. Words were exchanged with our thoughtless neighbour, and it has not happened again, so far. It appears that other neighbours had suffered from this for several years, but no one had spoken out before.

Although we didn't want to be bad neighbours, certain ground rules had to be established from the beginning, and this was one of them.

When we moved into our new home in Gran Canaria, we awoke one morning to the smell of smoke that made us choke. We had left the bedroom windows open over night as it was so hot, and we could see clouds of black smoke heading our way from the adjoining fields.

Unlike our Teignmouth neighbours who had remained quiet, our new neighbours were standing outside their gates chatting and complaining loudly to each other. We joined the group and quickly discovered that a tomato farmer who owned the adjoining field had a habit of burning the dying plants once the crop had been harvested.

Immediate complaints were made to the Town Hall by a self-appointed organiser, a police car arrived shortly afterwards, with two stern looking policemen sporting guns. The field of burning tomato plants gradually died down. This situation never happened again in the years that we lived on the island, the field was left bare of crops, and we understand that the farmer was heavily fined and threatened with imprisonment.

Our neighbours on the island did have occasional barbecues, but it was never the novelty that it is in the UK, presumably because the weather is always kind to the islands, and there is simply no need to make a big deal when the sun finally shines. Bonfires and incinerators were strictly forbidden on the islands, with heavy fines and penalties enforced if the rules were breached.

The ban on fires at home, including barbecues in forests, were heavily enforced for very good reasons. Not only were the islands' government aware of the threats of global warming and the responsibilities of all communities to play their part, but were also attempting to prevent yet another disastrous fire spreading in the bone-dry forests.

Parts of Gran Canaria, as well as its sister islands, were regular victims of forest fires that became quickly out of control. A few were started deliberately by arsonists, whilst others from illegal family barbecues that got out of hand. During our time on the island, entire communities lost their homes, livestock and crops and such events were always a major cause of worry to island communities.

There are some legal events involving bonfires and fireworks on the islands. One such event is the Feast of St John the Baptist that takes place during the evening of 23rd June. Lighting bonfires and setting off fireworks is traditional, with people dressed as devils carrying pitchforks with fireworks attached to them. These costumed devils dance to the heavy beat of drums as they set off their fireworks. We did witness this strange event once for an article that I was writing, but we quickly returned home as the night-time temperature was already in excess of 40 degrees. It always seemed to be a strange time of year to hold such an event when temperatures were already at their peak, and a bonfire was the last thing needed.

One common problem that plagues animal lovers in both Spain and the Canary Islands, as well as the UK are fireworks. It was not unusual to see children in the streets deliberately throwing fireworks at stray dogs, cats and other animals and David and I had to intervene on several occasions.

Before the recession hit the islands, letting off fireworks became a regular occurrence from the beginning of October to Halloween, through to Christmas and New Year. In addition, fireworks continued until at least the Day of the Three Kings on 6 January, and for some time thereafter and until supplies ran out. When the recession hit the islands in 2009/2010, it brought considerable hardship for many island people. The one positive thing that can be said for that troubling period was that there were few fireworks imported, bought and sold and the problem ceased for several years.

One serious event that should be mentioned were the volcanic eruptions that recently took place on the neighbouring island of La Palma. Lava from the volcano streamed down hillsides, and destroyed hundreds of homes, crops and animals. Thousands of people were evacuated and the future for many remained uncertain. Once volcanic lava reached the sea, noxious gases were expelled that are highly dangerous to health.

We used to visit La Palma regularly when we lived in Gran Canaria. We visited all eight inhabited islands regularly and in turn as part of our work for the newspaper, as well as for holidays and relaxation.

La Palma was one of our favourites; for the size of the island, it has a surprisingly large and well-equipped airport designed to deal with increasing numbers of international holidaymakers who were rapidly discovering this gem of an island, and for those wishing to escape the traditional resorts on the larger islands.

La Palma offers volcanic beauty, amazing seascapes, clean air and non-light polluted skies. The future of this island's main economy, tourism, is now threatened, as is growing crops such as bananas and pineapples. Despite this, there are possibly even more serious threats on the way that are of significance to us all.

There has been a theory for many years that a major volcanic eruption on the island of La Palma, would lead to the collapse of the western flank of the Cumbre Vieja volcano on the southern part of the island, which could create a powerful 50 metre 'mega tsunami' that could reach and sweep across the east coast of the USA, as well as other parts of the world.

Of course, experts tend to focus on the USA, but the dismissive reference to "other parts of the world" in various studies is likely to include the Bahamas, the Caribbean, and even reach parts of the UK and Europe, although it is assumed that waves would get smaller as they cross the Atlantic. This theory has been criticised and discounted by governments across the world many times over, no doubt to avoid mass panic. Despite this, arguments that this is very likely to happen are resurfacing once again.

Reassuringly, I am told that there is a greater chance of being killed in a car accident than by a mega-tsunami, since they are very rare. I hope that governments understand the potential risks, so that they can prepare for likely disaster scenarios, but I somehow doubt that such forward planning is likely in the UK.

On a more positive, but selfish note, I am relieved that we have left our home in Gran Canaria, which was very close to the beach, to live in our new home on a hill in Devon.

Charity Shops

This experience was in complete contrast to our time in Gran Canaria. In our neighbouring town of Vecindario, there were two charity shops. Both shops focussed on raising funds for those recovering from both drug and alcohol abuse, of which there are many cases throughout the islands.

My goodness, the staff working in charity shops in Devon are a picky lot! They certainly know how to stick their noses into the air, and reject items offered to them. I wonder if this is the same throughout the country? I hope not, because many good quality items that could be of use to someone will end up in landfill.

My first experience of charity shop rejection came when I had a handful of DVDs that I no longer wanted. I thought I would drop these into the local Oxfam shop. I was joined by an elderly woman who I had spotted staggering along the pavement carrying a large box of what looked like books.

We entered the shop together. As we both entered the shop, we were looked up and down by a plump middle-aged man who looked enquiring at the elderly woman and her box of books. He then glanced at me and my handful of DVDs, and then shook his head.

"Oh no. We are far too busy to sort them. We are inundated with the stuff. We cannot take them."

The elderly woman signed. "Oh no, I've just walked all the way from the car park with them. I hadn't realised how heavy they are. Some of these books are new. Are you sure you cannot take them?"

"Quite sure," was the offhand response, as he turned away and walked into a side room.

"Look, let me take the box of books, and you carry my DVDs," I offered. "Let's try the 'Cats' Protection' shop. They usually welcome most things."

The elderly woman gratefully swapped her heavy box of books for my DVDs and we walked together to an adjoining road, and walked into the 'Cats' Protection' shop. The greeting given was in complete contrast to that in the Oxfam shop, and the lady behind the counter gratefully accepted the box of books and my DVDs. She spotted one of them and put it to one side.

"I'll be buying that one for myself. I was hoping that would turn up one day. It will complete my Hardy collection," she smiled.

"Yes, I like Hardy too, I replied. "I already have one copy, but someone gave me that one as a gift some time ago, and I don't need two. It's a good film, I hope you enjoy it."

"I'm sure I will. Thank you both for the books and DVDs. They always sell well. We keep the prices low, but it all adds up and helps the cats."

I said goodbye to the friendly sales lady and to the elderly woman who was browsing the card section.

"Thank you for your help with the books. I'm going to buy my Christmas cards here. I have many more books at home, so I will bring them here instead of Oxfam in future." I nodded in agreement, and I also decided not to visit the Oxfam shop again.

This experience was in complete contrast to our time in Gran Canaria. In our neighbouring town of Vecindario, there were two charity shops. Both shops focussed on raising funds for those recovering from both drug and alcohol abuse, of which there are many cases throughout the islands.

The charities focussed on giving training and work opportunities to those in need, as a step towards helping them to regain their self-respect and sense of purpose. These charities did some excellent work, and on several occasions, we employed their workers to help remove trees and hedges that were no longer needed. We were never disappointed, and we were always pleased with their work. Both shops were also very grateful for anything offered to them. They would usually collect larger items the same day and I never knew them to reject anything offered to them.

We also bought several items of furniture ourselves from them, including a superb three door wardrobe. It was brand new and proved to be so useful that we brought it back with us to the UK for use in our garage. Local furniture and other companies often donated new and very good quality items that were at the end of the range or had minor damage.

Both shops became treasure troves for books, vinyl records, CDs and all things electrical. The stringent, and some would say excessive, health and safety rules that apply in the UK, didn't seem to apply on the islands, and so it was always important to have any electrical item tested for safety after purchase. These shops were ideal for browsing and always a good place to pick up a surprising bargain. How we miss them.

We support the UK's valuable hospice movement although, as with the RNLI, we believe that both organisations should be publicly funded and not have to rely upon charitable donations. It was with this in mind that I telephoned our local hospice to offer a nearly new bed and mattress, as well as a brand-new bed and mattress that were no longer required. The hospice told us that there would be a delay in collecting them as they were very busy, but they would let us know when they were passing. In the meantime, we stored the items in our garage.

I had bought both beds to see us through the anticipated several weeks delay when our container of possessions would be shipped from the islands to the UK. We were told that it could take up to two months before our belongings were delivered to our new home in Devon. Once our container arrived, we no longer had any need for the beds of which only one had been briefly used, since David was still in Gran Canaria dealing with that part of our relocation.

Two weeks later, I received a call from the hospice to say that they were passing the following morning. The van pulled into our driveway and two men walked over to the beds that were waiting for them. The older man shook his head and lit a cigarette. The irony that he worked for the hospice was not lost on me.

"We don't take mattresses. It's against the law."

I had heard something about UK charities not accepting mattresses, but I had assumed that since one was nearly new and the other still had plastic wrapping there would be some flexibility.

"You sure about that? That one has only been used for a couple of months and the other is brand new."

"Don't make any difference. Can't take 'em."

"Oh, what about the beds? Surely you can take those?"

"We could, if they were perfect. Look, both have got a scratch on the headboards. That counts as damage, we can't take 'em either."

I nearly exploded with anger, "That's the way Amazon delivered them. The beds are in perfect condition. If the scratch on the headboard is such a problem, it could be covered or changed for a different one."

"No, that's as may be, but we still can't take 'em' that counts as damaged goods," said the older man, as both walked back to their van and drove off.

Again, I made up my mind never to donate anything to the hospice again. Sadly, the council housing department were not at all interested either, despite the number of homeless people seeking accommodation in the area, as well as others who were desperate for household goods. Surely someone wanted two good beds? Apparently not, in the end I had to telephone a private contractor and pay them to take the beds to the dump, or recycling centre as it is now called. There is no wonder that fly tipping is such a problem in Devon.

Not all charities operate in the same way, and I am sure that there are others who would welcome good quality items to sell and raise money for their specific cause. Since that time, I have donated items to the British Heart Foundation and Age Concern without a problem, but other charity shops have shown a similar negative response to items offered to them. These experiences have reminded me of the difference between Spain, where there is real poverty and genuine need, and the level of need in the UK.

There are many in the UK that are in desperate need too, but I do wonder how well they are supported by some of the better-known charities, as well as local authorities who have such a negative attitude towards items offered to them, which could be of help. The term 'throwaway society" has never been clearer to me than my experiences of charity giving in the UK.

A Nice Cup of Tea

Looking around, I could see customers sadly eating their cream teas, sitting on stainless steel chairs, at stainless steel tables and drinking tea from plastic cups. This is not how I remembered cream teas at National Trust properties.

How I craved for a nice piece of cake! Peering through the beautifully displayed windows of patisserie shops in Gran Canaria, I knew from bitter experience that what I saw in the window did not reflect what it would taste like. Most of these delicacies appear to be made from a sickly, custard type concoction that looked good, but did not suit my taste.

I was very excited at the thought of having a traditional Devon cream tea at a nearby National Trust property. This would be my first for sixteen years, and the National Trust have a well-deserved reputation for serving high quality cakes, as well as excelling at cream teas.

Fine quality china, pleasantly designed and comfortable furnishings usually set in a beautifully converted barn or outdoor traditional building usually add to the experience. Maybe it was my memory playing tricks, but on this occasion, I was bitterly disappointed.

The tearoom at the National Trust property could be described as anything but traditional. It was a nod to a cheap looking, modern, utility design that was clearly designed to serve its purpose of dealing with mass footfall at low cost and minimal staffing requirements.

As I queued at the gleaming stainless-steel counter, I could see plates of freshly made scones on display behind the glass screen, accompanied by small jars of what I usually refer to as 'plastic jam' and small plastic pots of cream; it didn't look at all promising.

The cream tea was 'served' on a cardboard plate, accompanied by a plastic knife and a plastic spoon, covered with cling film. Looking around, I could see customers sadly eating their cream teas, sitting on stainless steel chairs, at stainless steel tables and drinking tea from plastic cups.

This is not how I remembered cream teas at National Trust properties. I dismissed the idea of a cream tea and ordered a packet of digestive biscuits and a bottle of water instead. I was bitterly disappointed. If anyone from National Trust Catering ever reads this, they will probably give their explanation as it was "It was all due to Covid (or Brexit)". It probably was due to Covid; however, the problem is that these things rarely return to as they were.

There is no doubt that these changes are designed to reduce staffing costs, increase footfall, reduce waste (if you ignore all the plastic packaging) and, above all, healthy increases in profit margins. Some clever, highly paid, cost cutting accountants will no doubt be clapping their hands with glee as they check their balance sheets and consider their bonuses. Meanwhile, we have lost another piece of tradition and much goodwill to this well-respected charity in the process.

Fortunately, my disappointment at my first attempt of enjoying a cream tea after a gap of sixteen years was quickly corrected when I visited one of many wonderful tea rooms in Teignmouth. Freshly made scones, lashing of homemade jam and clotted cream served on delicate plates, with beautiful cups and saucers to match. There was not a cardboard plate or cling film in sight, pure bliss! Back to that age-old question, does jam go on the scone first and then cream, or is it cream first and then the jam? The battle between Devon and Cornwall on this important, traditional matter continues, so I will decline to comment on this one, as I have a loyalty to both camps.

As I mentioned earlier, Spain and the Canary Islands have no shortage of patisseries, but few offer cakes and pastries that appeal to the British palette. It is doubtful if you will ever find anything like a Victoria sponge, almond slice, cream horn and chocolate eclairs unless you visit one of the many 'British Supermarkets' that appeared the across the country.

We were fortunate, since there is an excellent Marks and Spencer franchise on the island which, although expensive, was very useful whenever we wished to buy sweet or savoury treats. Other than this, we relied upon buying various tarts and pastries from the local supermarket, as well as bags of small muffins or 'magdalenas', which were often the closest that we could get to sponge cake.

Since returning to the UK, I have noticed that cupcakes have become very popular and appear to rival the traditional cream tea or slice of Victoria sponge. There is a very good tea shop in Teignmouth that specialises solely in cupcakes. These wonderful creations look almost too good to eat; the painstaking design and craftwork are amazing to see. I also attended a wedding recently where cupcakes replaced the traditional wedding cake, and very good they were too.

One celebration cake that I remember enjoying with good friends in Gran Canaria during the Christmas season was a kind of large cream-filled bun that we shared with friends on The Day of the Three Kings, which is on 6 January. Our 'cake' was simply decorated, but enthusiasts could also purchase much more elaborate versions. Interestingly, this traditional 'cake' also included a small crown and a dried bean somewhere inside.

The lucky finder of the crown would become King or Queen for the day, whilst the one who found (or unfortunately swallowed) the bean would be responsible for providing the King's Day cake the following year. I am quite sure that these cakes would be banned in the UK due to health and safety reasons.

In Gran Canaria, David and I always baked our own bread, albeit in a bread maker, which we had brought with us from the UK. When we arrived in Spain sixteen years ago, breadmaking machines were unheard of and it was impossible to buy one unless it was shipped across from the UK via Amazon.

Over time this situation changed, and the machines became very popular. Although bread flour and other ingredients were easy to find, yeast for bread makers was always an issue. Fortunately, my brother came to the rescue and would post supplies of dried yeast to us. In addition, visiting friends would often bring the supplies that we needed.

We rarely bought bread from shops and bakeries in Spain, simply because it didn't have the flavour that we were used to. However, Spanish patisseries were masters at making croissants, and these delicacies regularly became part of our mid-morning tradition, to be enjoyed with coffee. Despite not having the range of cakes and pastries that we were used to in the UK, donuts were much enjoyed by workers visiting bars for a snack during their breaktime.

Bright yellow packets of sticky, fatty and sugary donuts were always on display in café bars. These were produced by one company that also provided plastic display cabinets to further tempt customers with their sticky offerings. Donuts could easily be one of the reasons where residents of the Canary Islands, and children particular, suffered from one of the highest levels of obesity in Spain.

Despite all this talk about cakes and pastries I have, so far, not mentioned what we drank alongside these treats. Sadly, it was never tea. Despite many attempts to make a 'nice cup of tea', it was almost impossible to create. I know many visitors to Spain, as well as British immigrants living in Spain, who will confirm this disastrous aspect of life in Europe. Experiments with teabags purchased only in the UK, bottled water, spring water and tap water were all to no avail.

We initially believed that much of the problem was the use of desalinated water, which even when boiled still made a dreadful cup of tea. After many frustrating attempts, we gave up, and only drank coffee; life is just too short. Some of the best coffee that I have ever tasted was in the Canary Islands. It was always cheap, and rarely cost more than one euro per cup throughout our time living in the country.

It often amuses me when I contrast the simplicity of purchasing a delicious cup of coffee in Spain to that of the complexity, expense (and noise) when trying to buy a cup of coffee in Costa Lottee in the UK.

Overall, in my opinion, the UK certainly comes out top rated when it comes to the quality and imagination of its cakes, scones and pastries when compared to its Spanish counterparts. The many teashops in its high streets, stately homes and other venues bear witness to the British love of traditional teatimes, but at a price. I have noticed recently that these simple teatime treats are now often accompanied by a glass of champagne and plates of finely cut, cucumber sandwiches that would not look out of place when served at a Royal Garden Party.

From what I am told, 'a nice cup of tea' is out of the question in Spain, Italy, Greece, Germany and France and I suspect much of Europe. Although good quality coffee at a sensible price may not easily be available in the UK, the country simply cannot be beaten for 'a nice cup of tea'.

The Veggie Option

Many Spanish seemed to think that tuna is a plant and not a fish, which often led to misunderstandings

David and I have been vegetarian for most of our lives, with more recent years gradually attempting to be vegan, with a mixed degree of success. Although we both believe strongly that veganism is the way forward for both ourselves and the planet, we know that it is not a view commonly shared.

We go as far as we can personally, but avoid pushing our views onto others, unless they raise the issue. Pushing personal views onto others can do far more harm for the vegan cause than good. A vegetarian approach to life has never been easy for us, and certainly not when growing up within a carnivorous culture.

As a gay couple, we were often regarded as 'oddities' by both family and friends, and being vegetarian, as well as Quakers, certainly didn't help. There were those who didn't agree, but respected our views, whilst there were others who would make fun of our ideals and do their best to belittle us. Thankfully, although I didn't realise it at the time, this early training of argument, reasoning and defence was one of the reasons that I landed one of my early teaching roles.

I had been called for interview for the deputy headship of a Catholic school. As a non-Catholic, I assumed that I had been called merely to make up numbers, rather than being seriously considered for the job.

Initially, I was reluctant to attend, but later realised that it would be good experience for later applications, it would get me known by County Hall and, I am a little ashamed to add, would give me a rather pleasant day off, expenses paid, in another part of the county. Overall, it seemed as if I didn't have anything to lose and rather more to gain.

The early tour of the school went well, I liked the headteacher and staff, the children seemed happy enough, but lacking in self-discipline in corridors and the playground, and over controlled in the sterile and unimaginative classrooms. The modern building appealed to me, as I had previously taught in dark and draughty Victorian buildings, although I shuddered at the thought of having a statue of 'Joseph with the Bleeding Heart' stage centre in the classroom that I would presumably occupy if successful.

I immediately dismissed the thought as pointless, since I had already assumed any of the other five candidates could be appointed, as they were all 'true, blue Catholics'; as a Quaker, I didn't really didn't stand a chance.

The first round of interviews in the morning went well, or so I thought. I was well prepared and I could answer all of the questions that the headteacher, County advisors, Diocesan staff and governors could throw at me. At the end of the first round of interviews, three candidates were asked to leave and, to my surprise, myself and two others were asked to join the governors, headteacher and advisory staff for lunch.

These invitations to lunch were, of course, an obligatory part of the interview process, an old trick designed to check that we could hold our knives and forks correctly, and that candidates possessed the required social skills and good manners required for a church school. I had attended a couple of such events before and, knowing that I would not be a favoured candidate, was determined to enjoy my lunch and to be myself. After all, it was a day out and good experience.

The other two candidates and myself were shared between several governors and driven to a country hotel. There was a carefully constructed seating plan and I was allocated a seat between the Diocesan Education Advisor on my right and another candidate, Peter, to my left.

As soon as we were seated around the large circular table, a young waitress appeared offering non-alcoholic drinks, which was a pity as I was ready for a glass of wine.

I could both smell and sense that a roast meal was about to be served, and as the waitress offered me a glass of orange juice, I mentioned quietly to her that I was a vegetarian and could I just have the vegetables?

"No problem, would you like some cheese to go with it?" nodded the helpful young woman.

"Thank you. That would be lovely," I replied.

Peter suddenly joined in the conversation, "So you are a vegetarian then, are you?" he said in a loud voice. "That's a bit weird, isn't it? I guess you have to be very careful to get the right protein. I'm a big meat man myself," he announced proudly.

By now, everyone else had put down their glasses, stopped talking and were looking at Peter and myself.

"In the same way that we all have to balance what we eat. I try to live without other living beings having to die for my pleasure and nutrition."

"What nonsense!" exclaimed Peter loudly, keenly aware that our conversations were being listened to with great interest and, indeed, surprise. "Where did you find that in the Bible?"

"I'm not aware that it does, Peter. But I do know that God gave us free will, choice, and that we are custodians of all that is living."

Peter became angry and started firing more questions at me. Over the years, I have become highly practised at defending and standing up for the beliefs that are important to me.

Our arguments became livelier until we were interrupted by the Chair of Governors, the local priest, who skilfully changed the subject. I was happy to leave it there and was satisfied with my performance. On the other hand, I noticed that Peter had far more to say and looked dejected after being told 'enough is enough'.

At the end of the afternoon, I was offered the job as Deputy Headteacher of the Catholic School, and I was told by the County Education Advisor that it was very rare for a non-Catholic to be appointed, although such schools often went through the motions. I asked him how I had performed and the reasons for my appointment.

"It was your lunchtime debate with Peter. You handled the questions sensitively and passionately. It was a no brainer for all of the governors. They knew that you were the right man for the job by the end of the conversation."

I discovered later that Peter, a staunch Catholic and, as I discovered later, the son of a local butcher, had been appointed as deputy headteacher of a local Church of England School. We became the best of friends, and continued our lively discussions on the football field when our teams were playing against each other.

We knew that our move to Spain would bring with it many challenges, least of all the issues with food. Fortunately, David is a good and imaginative cook and we survived very nicely on the wonderful variety of fruit, vegetables and pulses that were easily and cheaply available at our local supermarket.

We avoided prepared products as our lack of understanding of the Spanish language could lead to problems in mistakenly buying and eating non-vegetarian ingredients. Our main problems came when eating out. Although delicious salads and omelettes were readily available, we could never be sure what had been added to 'liven' them up.

Often tuna or ham would be sprinkled over the salads, and the red pieces within the Spanish omelette that were supposed to be red pepper would turn out to be pieces of ham. Many Spanish seemed to think that tuna is a plant and not a fish, which often led to misunderstandings. As a result, our choice of café bars and restaurants became very limited and we would only frequent those that understood and respected our wishes.

Despite this, there were many positive discoveries, with one of best vegetarian restaurants that we have ever visited located in our nearest town of Torrevieja. This restaurant was a delight to visit, and it was heart-warming to know that it was always very popular and busy. Diners could only be guaranteed a table if they booked well in advance. Change was rapidly coming to Spain.

When we moved to the Canary Islands, we seemed to take several steps backwards. The islands seemed oblivious to changes in dietary attitudes, and through our work with the newspaper, we were aware of complaints and criticisms from holidaymakers regarding the range and choices of food on the islands.

Local delicacies, such as goat and rabbit stew were one thing, but other dietary needs had to be addressed if the islands were going to be success as an international tourist destination. Little by little, with gentle persuasion from the islands' government and tourism departments, we began to notice that menus were beginning to appear in languages other than Spanish, vegetarian and vegan options were being offered, as well as menus for those on a celiac diet.

Wholefood shops, also stocking a range of vegetarian products, began to appear and, by the time that we left the islands, it was unusual to find a restaurant that didn't attempt to offer some vegetarian dishes. We witnessed a period of considerable and welcome change in the islands' fortunes and much of this was due to changes in attitudes, and an acceptance and willingness to adapt to consumer demands.

Motoring in Spain

Problems usually arose because British residents had not done their homework, to become familiar with Spanish motoring laws and requirements, as well as failing to learn a little of the language and culture of their newly adopted country.

My first experience of driving on Spanish roads in the Costa Blanca was not nearly as frightening as I had been led to believe, but I rapidly concluded that it is not a good idea to drive a British right-hand drive car on Spanish roads. The right hand/left hand drive issue results in complications that I would much rather avoid, such as not being able to see clearly.

Fortunately, I ignored the macho comments made by many mainly male British drivers returning from a brief holiday on the continent, that "driving in Europe, on the wrong side of the road, is a piece of cake!" It certainly isn't, and I would not do it again. A Spanish car for Spanish roads was the only way forward.

One of my first jobs in the Costa Blanca was to deliver thousands of copies of a free local English language newspaper to numerous shops and bars. As we had no car, one of our new neighbours kindly let us borrow their British vehicle for a few weeks until we got ourselves organised with a new car.

That was easier said than done, since buying a new or used vehicle in Spain requires registering with the authorities to obtain the all-important identity card and number, which is essential for all transactions, legal and otherwise, in the country.

Getting the identity card usually meant a very early morning start to drive to Alicante, and wait in a long queue for hours in baking heat, but often being told to go away, since the daily allocation had been met. Despite attempting to do this for ourselves on several occasions, we finally gave up.

Once we had decided to purchase a new, basic car, a Hyundai Getz, which became our loyal and reliable friend for sixteen years, the salesman agreed to organise the identity card for us for a small fee, and on condition that we bought the car from him.

We agreed, and in a couple of days, David had his new shiny identity card which meant that we could finally purchase the Getz and deliver the newspapers without troubling our kind and thoughtful neighbours. The Hyundai Getz remains one of our all-time favourite cars, which looked after us safely and reliably until we returned to the UK.

For three days, we regarded it as our main home, since we had sold our villa in the Costa Blanca and were crossing the Atlantic on a three-day voyage to Gran Canaria with two dogs, essential luggage and a laptop computer ready to start our new job, to publish and launch a new English language newspaper in the Canary Islands.

We were very reluctant to finally say goodbye to the Getz, despite it having been around the clock twice in its sixteen years with us. The harsh sunlight had scorched much of its grey body work, which I had resprayed from time to time, and when we finally said goodbye, it looked as smart as the day that we had collected it from the showroom.

When we arrived back in the UK, we immediately started looking for a new car. Sadly, by then the Hyundai Getz was no longer in production, but we bought another Hyundai without any hesitation. This time it is a Hyundai i10, a model that reminds us so much of our much-loved Getz, although now an automatic model.

During my time as a newspaper reporter, I covered many stories involving the British and their regular brushes with the law. These were usually minor offences, but it always surprised me how indignant many of these 'minor criminals' were once discovered and charged.

I remember interviewing several Brits who approached me in the hope that a story in the newspaper would somehow absolve them from charges for parking offences, driving without a licence or insurance, or driving a car in non-roadworthy condition.

I remember asking several "Would you have done this in the UK?" My question was always met with a look of surprise, indignation and often arrogance; it was if, somehow, Spanish laws did not apply to them. Sadly, this arrogance and often ignorance, were two reasons why British people were not always welcome, despite their spending power from very favourable currency exchange rates at that time.

Problems usually arose because British residents had not done their homework, to become familiar with Spanish motoring laws and requirements, as well as failing to learn a little of the language and culture of their newly adopted country.

British drivers often have great trouble with roundabouts when driving in Spain and there were always many cases of British and Irish drivers driving in the wrong direction on a roundabout, often causing serious accidents. One memorable occasion was when our Town Hall in Gran Canaria decided to erect a lovely Christmas tree, complete with lights and decorations, in the centre of a roundabout just outside our village before Christmas.

It only lasted two days, because late one night, an intoxicated British driver drove into the tree in the middle of the roundabout. The car was a right off, the tree toppled over, but the driver escaped unhurt. Sadly, the Christmas tree was removed and no Christmas tree has appeared since.

For many months, David and I ignored the requirement to exchange our UK driving licences for a Spanish one. The duration of UK licences was longer than their Spanish equivalents, and we felt uneasy about parting with our UK licence, because it meant lengthy delays in the issue of a new Spanish licence. Since we had elderly relatives living in the UK, there was often a need to return to the UK at short notice when we would need to hire a car and show a current licence.

When we arrived in Gran Canaria, it was clear that we could no longer avoid the driving licence requirements. Since I was regularly writing newspaper articles about driving in Spain, it was clear that my ignorance of the law would not be accepted as an excuse. David and I drove to the office responsible for all things to do with vehicles, Trafico, where an angry looking man glanced quickly at our UK driving licences and abruptly dismissed us with a flick of his hand.

"Not necessary to change. The UK is in Europe, and you have a European licence." We left, very pleased, but quite sure that the surly official was wrong. Our sixteen years ended with both of us still holding UK driving licences, which we were pleased to have retained for our return to the UK.

It was also important for us to have the driving licence, because it had to be used as an identity document when applying for essential services in the UK.

One thing that we appreciate about motorists in Devon is how courteous most are when driving. There are many very narrow and almost unpassable roads and lanes in the county, and unless one drives with great care and consideration for others accidents are bound to occur.

I am often pleasantly surprised by the way in which others will stop, wait and wave me on when trying to overtake a parked vehicle or entry onto a busy road. There are exceptions to this, of course, but it's a thumbs up from me for most Devon drivers!

I contrast these recent experiences with driving on busy Spanish roads and motorways. It is very much a 'me first' mentality, although I suspect that many guilty drivers are tourists, and not Spanish or Canarian residents.

Needless to say, Brexit continues to have far-reaching, negative consequences for British motorists living in Spain. At the time of writing, Spain has banned British residents from driving in the country, following a dispute with the UK government over a post Brexit plan on driving licences.

Simply exchanging a UK licence for a Spanish one is no longer possible, and those affected by the new ruling will have to study and take a driving test in Spain in order to obtain a Spanish driving licence before being allowed back on the roads.

Once again, the Brexit agreement has resulted in yet more expense, inconvenience and disappointment for British people living in Europe. One can almost feel the anger and indignant cries from Brits discussing the issue in Spanish bars! Sadly, quite a few of them also voted for Brexit!

Bills, Bills, and More Bills

Throughout our time in Spain and the Canary Islands, we only dealt with one company for electricity, water and telephone. Looking back, it was all so refreshingly simple and government could intervene as and when necessary to regulate prices and subsidise as necessary.

The Thatcher era taught us many things, the legacy of which lives on today. She and her government taught her followers the price of everything and the value of nothing. It was during Thatcher's watch that the mantra of 'the free market is everything' and 'there's no such thing as society'; this was utter rubbish of course, but Daily Mail readers believed her and many continue to do so. Competition became common currency and became widely accepted by much of the population.

Today, you don't have to be a socialist or an economist to notice that the free market is not working and many within the population are suffering as a direct consequence of a basically flawed philosophy. The free market may work successfully during times of prosperity and economic growth, but fails to address the needs of the wider population during times of crisis, such as the global recession, the Covid 19 pandemic, Brexit, and huge issues such as global warming, the war in Ukraine and the current energy crisis. It is during these periods where the less fortunate members of society become more vulnerable, which competition and the 'free market' are unable to fix.

'Privatisation' became a favourite mantra during both the Thatcher and Blair administrations. During the Thatcher era, particularly, much of the UK's 'crown jewels' were sold off to the highest bidder. In keeping with the competition and 'free market' philosophy, our electricity and telephone companies were privatised, together with the water company and British Rail. Many of the wealthier members of society were quietly complicit, since they were given the opportunity to buy shares at knock down prices, which many sold later for considerable financial gain.

It was a time when greed was encouraged, but was also a clever move on the part of the government, since those benefitting from generous share allocations were unlikely to complain. Just before David and I were to leave the UK for Spain, we began to see the flawed results of the new privatisation era.

Several new energy companies were established at great speed and we soon saw enthusiastic, young salespersons knocking on doors, asking householders to sign up to gas and electricity from these new companies. Water was slightly different, since it was only possible to create one private company, but the principle was broadly the same. It was all very confusing and difficult for some of the older members of UK society to understand.

Still, many had voted for Thatcher, so she must be right, and particularly after the Falkland's War. I sometimes wonder if Thatcher and her government would come to the same 'free market' conclusions when faced with the 2022 energy crisis?

Life was so much simpler in Spain. We had the choice of only one government-owned company for electricity, water and telephone. Admittedly, it took quite a lot of typical, slow moving Spanish bureaucracy and paperwork to get the connections, and we had to wait several months waiting our turn before we could get a home telephone connection, but we managed it in the end.

Our main problem with the electricity supply in Gran Canaria was reliability of the connection. Sometimes we would have a reliable supply for several weeks; it would then fail and we would have no supply for several hours. On occasions, the supply would come on and off several times a day, which is really not good for electrical appliances, such as washing machines and refrigerators. In our case, it was even more annoying, since we had no power for the computers, which could be critical close to publication deadlines for our newspaper.

Over time, we became adept at working on laptops with a backup battery supply, using portable modems and, in a real emergency, driving to the nearest commercial centre to work until the electricity supply was restored. Since most of our neighbours worked away from home, it was rare that anyone else noticed the problem until they returned home from work and noticed that their fridges were not working.

It was at this point that we realised that this was the trigger for our connection to be restored. We finally deduced that the problem stemmed from the control box at the end of our road, closest to the sea. It was clearly marked with 'no entry' and 'dangerous, do not enter' signs (in Spanish, of course). We began to watch the control box carefully, and it seemed that if someone from the electricity company did not arrive to switch us back on, one of our neighbours would do the job for them. It was on one of these occasions that David followed one of our neighbours to the box and asked him what he did to restore the power supply.

It was all quite simple, but the opposite of Spain's usual safety rules. David was told to press the red button to turn the power on, and the green button to turn it off. From that point onwards, whenever the power supply failed, David would walk to the connection box and press the red button.

Although ourselves and others complained to the electricity company many times, nothing was done. It was only at around the time that we were returning to the UK, and following an angry public meeting, the electricity company finally admitted that the problem was corrosion within the supply cabinet, which had been installed far too close to the sea. The electricity company agreed to replace it, although I do not know if this was ever done.

Some may think that our electricity bills on the island would have been very low, because of the favourable climate; they were not. We were faced with the same situation, but in reverse to householder's experience in the UK. During the summer months, it was often far too hot and as temperatures headed towards 40 degrees, it was essential to switch on air conditioning.

We had air conditioning units fitted in all rooms and they were regularly used during the summer months. Temperatures were very kind during the winter months and all that would be needed during the chilly winter evenings would be the warmth from one candle or, at worst, a one bar electric fire that made us feel warm simply by looking at it. Due to the expense of air conditioning, our electricity bills were similar to those for central heating in the UK.

Our water was metered and since it came from either the island underground springs or desalinated from seawater, it could not be relied upon for drinking. Although it was perfectly safe to drink from the tap, most people used bottled mineral water for their drinking supply. We had large plastic bottles of spring water delivered to our door each week, which saved carrying heavy supplies from our local supermarket.

Our bi monthly bills were high, and made us very careful when watering the garden as our supply was metered. I suspect that this was one of the reasons why few of our neighbours bothered to maintain a garden, and preferred instead to cover it entirely with tiles.

A pot with a plant would occasionally appear, which would not be watered, and would wither and die a couple of weeks later. Even though we only grew a few roses, lavender and, of course the inevitable cactus, neighbours would often comment about the extravagance of watering our small garden. As garden lovers, we could not imagine living in a house without outdoor plants.

Returning to the UK, one of my first jobs was to arrange for gas, electricity and water to be connected. I had not realised that to have an account with one of these companies one had to have a credit history. Of course, I did not have a UK credit history, although I had a good one, with credit and bank cards to match, in Spain, but this meant nothing in the UK. This was not acceptable and for a day or two it looked as if I would have to have prepayment electricity and gas meters installed until I had a provable UK credit history.

I was also shocked to discover that I was not eligible for a UK credit card, although we had maintained an account with the same UK bank for many years. The computer said "No" until I had been in the country for three years, was on the electoral roll, and had funds paid into our UK bank account.

Over the years, I have learned that there is always a way around foolish bureaucracy and the UK's now all-powerful credit agencies are no exception. I will never take "no" for an answer, and this problem was a relatively simple matter to get around. I had a new UK credit card within two weeks and connection to gas, electricity, water and telephone shortly afterwards. I was also learning that I had to check out deals with a multitude of these new energy companies.

I had neither the time, energy or the inclination when I had so many more important things to do, so went with the one that the previous occupant of our new property had used. I later regretted this and 'switched' to another, which was the first and possible last time that I will do this for reasons that I will explain later.

It was also irritating to discover that despite having a full no claim bonus on our car insurance policy in Spain, and no accidents, this was not acceptable in the UK. Even more surprising, the same company, Direct Line (Linea Directa in Spain), refused to acknowledge the Spanish no claim bonus in the UK. Needless to say, I changed to another insurance company, but still only managed to get a small 'beginners' discount in the UK.

Throughout our time in Spain and the Canary Islands, we only dealt with one company for electricity, water and telephone. Looking back, it was all so refreshingly simple and government could intervene as and when necessary to regulate prices and subsidise as necessary.

I contrast this to the current situation in the UK where global pressures on the price of energy have forced many energy companies out of business. Customers are then allocated another provider, for which they have no choice, and no control over the prices that they are charged with the new company.

Similarly, water companies in the UK are currently being criticised for disposing of untreated sewage in the rivers and seas during periods of heavy rainfall. Profits are being passed on to company directors and shareholders that should be reinvested in the network to ensure that this environmental vandalism does not continue. Thatcher's competition 'revolution' may have resulted in hefty gains for the City and corporate investors, but has done very little to improve investment and the renewal of facilities that are so badly outdated and in need of improvement.

Amazingly, our annual bill from the Town Hall, which is broadly equivalent to the UK's council tax, was about the same as we currently pay each month to our local council in Devon. In Gran Canaria, we had our roads and pavements swept daily, drains were emptied and jet washed, damaged pavements repaired, together with all manner of good local services that were there when needed.

As I have commented elsewhere, I have yet to be aware of similar attempts to clean roads and pavements, repair pavements and fill potholes in Devon, although I am sure that the council is very busy with a range of other services for its residents. It remains a mystery to me how our community in Gran Canaria enjoyed so much for so little, whilst there is very little evidence to justify the large monthly contributions that we make to our local council in Devon.

Another change stemming from the Thatcher era was the privatisation of the railway network. On the few occasions that I have attempted a journey by rail in the UK, I have been surprised by how difficult it is to purchase a ticket when travelling from A to B, and the confusing range of discounts and times with different train companies. It was worrying to discover that even though the traveller has managed to get a ticket to travel, this is restricted to a specific train company at a pre-determined time.

I had one such difficult journey when travelling to the North of the UK from London, when I inadvertently got on the wrong train belonging to the wrong company, even though it was going to the same destination, but a few minutes earlier. Despite a lively argument with the ticket collector, I had to pay for the entire journey again, but without the discount that I had gained earlier.

There are no trains to worry about in Gran Canaria, although the idea has been discussed several times in order to rapidly transfer passengers arriving on cruise ships in the Port of Las Palmas to the popular tourist areas in the south of the island. Despite attending endless press conferences, viewing mock ups of trains and carriages and the spouting of endless hot air, nothing has been done. I doubt Gran Canaria will ever have a train service, but it always makes good electioneering material.

Train services in Peninsular Spain, France and much of Europe are efficient, clean and usually very good value. Interestingly, the UK is one of the few countries that has privatised its train services, whilst they are mostly government owned in the rest of Europe.

Returning to the UK, it has been interesting to see the recent chaos on several of the UK's train services, with two of the train companies failing to meet their contractual commitments. Their services were duly renationalised by the UK government and are currently operated by a government agency; maybe this is the way forward? I have a helpful suggestion for the government, how about bringing all the train services together, and calling the new national service British Rail?

Pets and Vets

We were also very fortunate to have access to an excellent veterinary hospital on the island. This hospital was never intended to be a first port of call for minor illness, but only when an independent vet recommended it.

For most animal lovers, registering their pets with a good vet is an essential part of caring for them. Finding a good vet in the UK was one of my first jobs when I returned to the UK, even before registering David and myself with a good surgery and dental practice in town. It was not as easy I thought.

As most experienced parents discover when choosing a school for their child, they quickly sense whether a particular school is the right one when they visit, even for a short time. For me, it is the same with veterinary surgeries. I visited six in the immediate area, which ranged from excellent to 'needing improvement'. As an ex-school inspector, it was hard to avoid grading them.

One surgery was dirty and needed a thorough clean, the second had a receptionist that was so busy chatting up a visiting engineer that she couldn't even be bothered to acknowledge my presence.

The third was a busy one, which had a very small waiting area with several owners and a mixture of cats, dogs and a rabbit. This is not a good idea, as not all cats get on with dogs, and many dogs do not like cats; I felt very sorry for the rabbit. The fourth surgery was friendly enough, but seemed preoccupied with telling me about their pricing structure than the actual care and facilities available.

I was finally narrowed down to two surgeries, both of which seemed excellent. Ideally, I like to see very clean premises, separate waiting areas for dogs and cats and a receptionist who knows what she/he is talking about, and not acting as a human barrier between the client and the vet.

It was very hard to decide between the two surgeries and I made second visits to both of them, asking more questions, and collecting details of services, pricing, opening hours and all the other things that are so important if a dog or cat is in distress and needs prompt attention. It was very hard to decide as both surgeries were excellent.

In the end, I went with one that went entirely against my earlier views and expectations. I always said that I would never use a veterinary surgery that is attached to a pet supplies supermarket. Apart from excellent facilities, separate waiting areas for cats and dogs, there were several vets available that meant that the surgery offered long opening hours, even on Sundays.

The determining factor was being offered to speak to a vet by a charming and knowledgeable receptionist, and whilst waiting, observing the manner that patients were welcomed from the moment they entered the surgery until the time that they left. It was time well spent; I had made up my mind and, so far, have not regretted my decision.

The choices were more limited in Spain and the Canary Islands. Many veterinary practices were operated by just one vet, which was troubling in cases of emergency or when the vet was sick or wanted to go on holiday.

Our little dog, Bella, a short-tempered Spanish girl at the best of times, took an instant dislike to one very kind lady vet called Rita. Rita's problem was that she was just too 'gushing', which Bella immediately saw through. It was Rita who spayed Bella, which Bella never forgave, and insisted upon giving Rita a really rough time whenever they came in contact with each other.

Manuel, a quiet and sensitive older man operated a one-man surgery in the Canary Islands. Bella took to him immediately and never gave him any problems. Manuel didn't make an excessive fuss of her, and his calm, quiet and reassuring manner was just what Bella responded well to.

Sadly, it was Manuel who correctly diagnosed a serious heart condition in our corgi, Barney. Barney had developed a bad, continuous cough. Manuel quickly and correctly diagnosed the condition, which we could see was serious from his expression and few, kind words. Barney passed away quietly in David's arms a few days later.

One of the most frightening things about vets in the UK is the size of their bills. Before our move to Spain, we remember some very large bills being presented at the end of a veterinary consultation. I still remember the comments of surprise and anger when receptionists presented the bill to clients who had not had the good sense to check the likely costs of consultations, surgery and treatments. In fairness, this is often the last thing that pet owners consider if they have a much-loved pet in distress, but this is a time when, in some cases, pet owners are most likely to be exploited.

In contrast, the vet practices in the Canary Islands offered a very fair pricing structure. It was unusual to pay more that 40 euros for a consultation, which would often include the drugs. Any repeat visits were usually free of charge if linked to the first condition.

As a result of fair charging, pet owners were far more likely to bring their pets for treatment, knowing that the charges would not be exorbitant. The policy on drugs was also a revelation.

Instead of prescribing very expensive drugs specifically designed for the veterinary market, most vets wrote a special veterinary prescription that clients could take to their local pharmacy. Many of the drugs prescribed for pets are similar to those prescribed for humans, but at a much lower strength. As a result, the cost of prescribed drugs for animals was many times lower in Spain than the expensive drugs, specifically designed for animals, prescribed by vets in the UK.

Veterinary care in Spain and the Canary Islands was generally excellent, with the exception of one very troubling experience where British immigrants were clearly seen as a generous source of funds to be exploited.

Our little dog Bella, a lively, and slightly crazy mixture of something between a Papillion and fruit bat, developed a bad limp in one her back legs. We were not too concerned at first, since the problem tended to occur every six months or so. We were convinced that somehow it was linked to her menstruation cycle. Usually, the bad leg returned to normal after a week of rest.

This time the problem continued and we took Bella to the vet for an anti-inflammatory injection or tablets, which usually did the trick. The helpful young vet gave her a thorough examination and it was clear after all the probing and prodding that Bella was not in any pain.

The vet also suggested that he took a couple of X-rays to make sure that all was in order. The X-rays showed inflammation and the vet confirmed that there were no fractures and all was fine. We were to give Bella a pill over each of the next three days, and after paying a bill of 100 euros later we left.

Four days later we returned to the surgery as instructed for a check-up. By then Bella was much better, she still had a slight limp, but was much improved. As soon as we entered the treatment room, another vet, a woman who we had not seen before, gave Bella a quick glance from her stool by the desk and immediately declared that Bella would need an operation. We were puzzled as the X-rays had shown no signs of a problem and this had been confirmed by the first vet.

"Oh, we often get this problem with small dogs like her," she huffed, tapping on her computer keyboard, and ignored our comments about it happening twice each year. Bella was given a rather more thorough examination by a second vet and he nodded in agreement.

We were then asked to see the traumatologist. When he arrived, Bella was given more prods and pokes and he confidently confirmed the diagnosis of the other two vets. We stood in white-faced silence as the woman vet continued to tap enthusiastically on her keyboard, whilst making that sharp sucking in of breath sound that I do so detest in Spain - it always means trouble.

We then entered the frightening world of surgery - complete with anaesthetics, drugs, treatment and recovery times. Did we also want specialist heart and blood tests before the operation? she barked. We were told that this was essential in case Bella was not fit enough and would die during the operation.

"That will be 800 euros, but you can pay over three months", she smiled, handing us the detailed printed estimate. "Oh, and by the way, she will also need the second leg doing as well, so shall we call it 1600 euros for the two?"

As a parting short, we were then told that it was important for Bella to take a special, and expensive, pill lasting two weeks until the time of her operation. Each pill cost 13 euros - we bought one and drove home in silence. We both felt uneasy because what we had just heard just was not convincing and contradicted the findings of the first vet.

Two weeks later, and after plenty of rest with restricted walks, Bella's leg fully recovered. We did not give her that expensive pill nor did she have the operations. It is now clear to us that these vets saw us as pet-loving Brits ready to hand over 1600 euros, at the expense of Bella's well-being.

Just as with human health, alternatives, therapies and drugs should always be considered before surgery. In Bella's case, the diagnosis for unnecessary surgery would have led to great expense and treatment that would have caused her pain and distress for several months. Needless to say, we immediately changed vets.

We were also very fortunate to have access to an excellent veterinary hospital on the island. This hospital was never intended to be a first port of call for minor illness, but only when an independent vet recommended it. In Bella's case, a troubling eye ulcer had to be dealt with and our vet rightly suspected other more serious conditions.

We visited the veterinary hospital on several occasions. It was a teaching hospital linked to the university and the highly qualified attending vets were always accompanied by a group of student vets who would assist in the procedure. Despite the fact that Bella never took prisoners, and took an instant dislike to the woman specialist who had the audacity to peer too closely into her poorly eyes, each visit was highly professional, kind and attentive. Bella was given first class care, which enabled her to enjoy a better quality of life and for us to share a few more valuable months with her.

Fortunately, both the UK and Spain offer very good veterinary care, but the main difference is the charges made. In Spain, it is rare to see pet insurance policies being advertised. They do exist, but are quite hard to find. When we lived in the Canary Islands, we bought such a policy for Bella and our cat, Mac.

It was surprisingly good value and came into its own during lengthy spells of expensive treatment for Bella. Pet insurance policies are heavily advertised in the UK; a similar policy in the UK for our dog, Oscar, and cat, Merlin, now costs many times more for restricted cover than our Spanish policy. Once again, these high costs are directly related to the very high veterinary treatment and drug costs in the UK when compared to those in Spain.

Something is rotten in the state of Denmark

We seem to have slipped into an alternative universe. It wasn't good when I left, but the lunatics now seem to have taken over the asylum.

"Something is rotten in the state of Denmark" is line that is spoken by Marcellus in Shakespeare's play, Hamlet, as he and Horatio debate whether or not to follow Hamlet and the ghost into the dark night. Marcellus is talking not only about Denmark's relationship with Norway, but is also summing up Claudius' corrupting effect on the kingdom, which is intensified by his unpunished crime.

Does this remind you of anyone in current British political circles? If it does, you will know what I am referring to without explanation or comment. If not, you really shouldn't be reading this book.

I should make it clear that my comments come from a left wing, pro Remain standpoint with an intense dislike of Johnson, Truss and their kind, as well as the current dysfunctional Conservative government. I should apologise if this chapter appears to be overly political. I have tried hard to avoid letting my own political ideals influence my observations, but as a keen observer of current affairs in the UK from an island in the Atlantic, it is hard not to.

My initial confirmation about how rapidly politics had deteriorated in the UK were confirmed by a chance meeting with a good friend and ex colleague, Anne, who had been living in France for over twenty years. Like ourselves, she had returned to the UK following the Brexit vote, and was clearly not happy about the situation that she now found herself in.

Anne sighed as the waitress placed a large cup of coffee in front of her and glared at me, "What has happened to this country, Barrie? Is it just me? I seem to be the only one who has noticed that the country has been taken over by morons. No one seems to notice or is prepared to do anything? We seem to have slipped into an alternative universe. It wasn't good when I left, but the lunatics now seem to have taken over the asylum."

I nodded. Maybe it wasn't the language that I would have chosen to describe the new state of affairs, but I knew exactly what Anne meant.

"Yes, my thoughts exactly. I think the country has been so taken up with the Brexit saga for so many years; the lies and deceit seem to have become the new normal. You are right, I don't think most people notice, unless they have been out of the country for a while. Most people seem to be too busy to care, and if they do notice they take the view that they cannot do anything about it anyway."

From an early age, Prime Minister Johnson announced that he wanted to be 'King of the World'. My own experiences with young children tell me that most want to be firemen, nurses, footballers and maybe princesses.

Admittedly, I did meet one talkative four-year-old who told me that she wanted to be an angel. Without delving too far into the theology and practicality of the suggestion, I pointed out that if she wanted to help people, maybe she could become a doctor or nurse as the first step to becoming an angel? The little girl thought for a moment, looked at me, and nodded. "I'll do that first then" she muttered stabbing a pair of blunt scissors into a lump of playdough.

As our previous Prime Minister floundered, blustered and burbled at a time of crisis, it may be worth pondering what exactly propelled the UK into this state of affairs from the viewpoint of an observer watching developments from a small island in the Atlantic.

Arriving back in the UK, I wondered why nearly everyone that I met referred to Johnson fondly as 'Boris', almost as if they knew him personally. I had to keep my mouth firmly buttoned when in conversation with some of our new neighbours. I do not recall Cameron or Blair being referred to as 'David' or 'Tony' by the general public, although I do remember Thatcher being called 'Maggie', but only in a derogatory sense at the end of her reign.

Whatever Johnson's faults, and he is deeply flawed human being, he does have the skills, carefully honed at Eton and Oxford University, whereby he can quickly ingratiate himself with anyone that he meets, and particularly those who cannot see through the act.

Part of this is, of course, playing the fool and the art of self-deprecation. Even when Johnson goes too far with his antics, Johnson lovers merely smile and say "Oh that's just Boris".

In reality, the Johnson act is carefully crafted; it is cultivated eccentricity, the Churchillian walk and the carefully coiffured 'Worzel Gummidge' hair are all designed to instil a 'man of the people' image to his admirers. Although Johnson is not particularly bright, he does possess native wit, and an Eton College charm. If all else fails, Johnson will try to impress with the odd quote in Latin, which he knows that most of his fans will not understand. "Surely such a fool cannot be truly dangerous?"

Despite the act, Johnson is not a fool, but a calculating performer who craves attention and is desperately in need of therapy. Such men are ultimately dangerous, both to themselves, as well as to others. These are also the kind of people who are easily manipulated by others, yet there are more sinister puppeteers who are pulling the strings.

Boris Alexander de Pfeffel Johnson, is not the cause of the problem. He is merely a symptom of a pervasive condition, a puppet carefully crafted to fulfil the ambitions of a small, but effective Europe-hating London-centred elite. Johnson, like so many attending that odious bastion of privilege, Eton College, and later Oxford, Johnson was bred to lead. It is not so much the direct fault of these institutions, but the sense of entitlement that they instil in some students.

An exaggerated sense of self-importance and disinterest in those that are less fortunate are disturbing, given than many of these privileged young men and women will eventually become Members of Parliament, Government ministers, lawyers and the like.

Johnson's antics with his fellow student, David Cameron, and other students at Oxford reportedly included trashing dining rooms, as members of the infamous Bullingdon Club, and burning twenty-pound notes in the faces of homeless people. Given their compassion shown as students, there is no wonder that Johnson currently presides over a cabal of similar misfits. As a result, there is widespread poverty, and social care and homelessness are in crisis, and the growing number of food banks in the country knows no bounds.

It is said that Johnson currently craves the downfall of his replacement, Truss, in the hope that he can make a 'Churchillian comeback'. Fortunately, I think that the lure of lucrative fees for his lecture tours in the US makes this unlikely.

Politics in Spain's Costa Blanca proved to be an enlightening experience. Looking back, I remember discussing Spain's PSOE (Socialist) party's election manifesto with friends several years later. In my experience of politics, it was the only political manifesto in both the UK and Spain where all the stated policies had been fulfilled - an amazing feat that I have not been aware of since. This manifesto bravely declared a commitment to civil partnerships for gay men and women, which was one of the first in Europe.

Sadly, it was an influx of British immigrants that began to stir up trouble in the Costa Blanca. As a new reporter, I was sent to cover a meeting at the local community hall where a large group of British immigrants were complaining that their views were either ignored or not represented on the municipal council.

I recall listening to this meeting, feeling acutely embarrassed, since most of the comments made were anti-Spanish, making unrealistic demands including providing free interpreters in any official building, free language classes, together with a range of other demands. There was very limited understanding or wish to learn and understand the Spanish language and culture.

Later, I interviewed a dogmatic, talkative, and, frankly, odious elderly man who had established himself as the spokesman for this British collective of unhappy souls. It was an unpleasant interview, and I found it very difficult to write a positive article for the newspaper afterwards. I left the interview wondering why he and his band of troubled followers bothered to live in Spain in the first place.

This self-proclaimed leader of unhappy Brits was eventually elected as a councillor at the next local election, as were many other British immigrants in subsequent elections. This was at the time when back in the UK, there was considerable unhappiness in the town of Boston, Lincolnshire where the local population were objecting strongly to the large influx of Polish immigrants into the town. I wondered how they would feel if Polish immigrants managed to get themselves elected as local councillors?

In the Costa Blanca, not only did British immigrants manage to infiltrate local councils, but in one nearby municipality a British mayor was elected. I do not recall how successful this appointee was in his new position but, again, reflected upon how well this would go down in Boston, should a Polish mayor ever be elected.

These were the beginning of troubled times, and I could begin to sense the resentment of some Spanish people to the negative impact that some British immigrants were having upon their communities. It was apparent that many, but not all, British immigrants were interested in a life of sipping gin and tonic in their new homes in the sun, with little regard to their new local communities.

Many were unwilling to learn the language or understand the culture, demanded similar facilities to those that they were used to "at home" and were only really happy drinking in 'British pubs' and buying overpriced British products in 'British' supermarkets.

Again, would the British really stand for this kind of behaviour should the position be reversed with immigrants living in the UK? I doubt it. I often wonder how the Spanish tolerate such interference in their affairs?

When we arrived in the Canary Islands, I remember that much of my time as a newspaper reporter was covering events for political parties that were working for the sole aim of the Canary Islands breaking away from Spain and becoming an independent country. Initially, this was alarming, but I soon realised that although the islands had both the political will and possibly the capacity to go it alone, I had serious doubts whether their economy could cope with the break from Spain.

Clearly, others soon felt the same, and over the next few years, I noticed that demands for full independence quickly faded. Spain, wisely, ensured that its regions become self-governing autonomous communities, but remaining within the protection and support of the Spanish state.

For most regions, this was sufficient, but several regions such as Catalonia and the Basque country had other ideas, which seriously challenged the patience of any Spanish government. In some cases, this led to serious civil disobedience and violence.

Politics in the Canary Islands never seemed to be taken too seriously. As European citizens, we were entitled to vote in municipal and European elections, but not National elections. Voting in our local polling station was always a fascinating event and a good excuse for a morning of entertainment, as well, as the more serious business of voting, of course.

The local primary school in our village was usually deployed for this important task, with voting always taking place on Sundays. Hordes of villagers gathered both inside and inside the polling station, chatting and laughing; some even brought picnics and could be seen sitting on seats outside the school chatting, and having an enjoyable time with their friends and neighbours.

For ourselves, it was all initially quite bewildering, but we were soon led to the correct voting area by helpful police officers, who were also clearly enjoying their day out, and were able to cast our votes.

We also managed to catch up with some of our neighbours, and by the end of the morning felt fully integrated into the ways of the voting Spanish public.
As a bonus, this was one of the few opportunities that we had to look around the school. As ex-teachers it was a welcome and fascinating experience to wander around what appeared to be a well organised, well equipped and attractive school.

Several years ago, the brilliant playwright, Russell T Davies wrote an extraordinary screenplay called 'Years and Years'. This six-part drama takes a look at a fictionalised version of current affairs through the eyes of a family in Manchester over the course of a 15-year period.

In this drama, society becomes more dysfunctional, and the turmoil of politics, technology and distant wars affects the family in their day-to-day lives. Britain withdraws from Europe, America becomes a lone wolf, China asserts itself, and a new world order begins to form.

The biggest danger to their well-being is a Trumpian styled MP, who is currying favour with an increasingly disenfranchised population. I recommend this series to anyone who has not seen it to do so if they wish to truly understand what is happening in Johnson's Britain. The parallels with reality are alarming.

The Banking Business

It was a heady time, and there was a strong positive feeling that the doors of a previously closed, often repressive and grey UK had suddenly opened to reveal a glimpse of a sunny and happier world.

Similar to many people, I have a love/hate relationship with banks, whether it be in the UK or Spain. Yes, when we need a mortgage, credit card or a loan to buy something special, they are useful, but few people aren't under any illusion that banks are here for one purpose only, and that is to make money for its directors and shareholders and rarely for the public good.

In recent years, we have become increasingly aware of the control that banks have over the direction of a country, as well as over the lives of the general public. The 2008 financial crisis was a wakeup call for both the industry and the general public. Wise governments saw to it that the banking sector was reformed and that individuals who had assisted in the worst effects of the crisis received justice.

In the UK, steps were taken to reform the worst effects of the crisis, and several banks and their mortgage portfolios were taken into public ownership, but I am not aware of any individuals that faced the justice that they deserved for the part that they played in the crisis.

In Spain, much of the cause of the financial crisis was the housing bubble, and its rapid unsustainable growth. In some ways, it began as a story of success, but poor supervision by the Spanish Government, the hiding of true financial positions by the banking sector, and ignoring regulations all led to a collapse of a sector that the Spanish Government was unable to help. As a result, Spain turned to the European Union for 100 billion euros in loans. The collapse of the financial sector was devastating, which led to massive unemployment, bankruptcies and recession.

This instability in Spain's fortunes came several years after our move to Spain. There was a massive building programme, which led to reasonably priced homes in the Costas being actively promoted to British and other European buyers, who were anxious to establish their own 'homes in the sun'.

Television programmes in the UK included popular series, such as 'A Home in the Sun' which promoted the idea and relatively simplicity of buying one of the many new build developments in Spain, France and elsewhere. In the UK, there were many families who had seen their own homes rapidly increase in value, which allowed for equity to be withdrawn to buy a second property in Europe.

We knew a number of people who had bought their council properties at a knock down price, a foolish policy of the Thatcher Government, and were now able to make a generous profit that enabled them to buy their dream home in the sun.

Sadly, new social housing to replace those that were sold under the Thatcher scheme didn't materialise, which is one of the many reasons why the UK currently has a serious housing crisis. For the intending buyer, everything looked rosy. As well as a plentiful supply of good value properties in a warm, sunny climate, the pound-euro exchange rate worked very generously in favour of those with pounds in their pockets. It was possible to live comfortably in Spain in a way that was much cheaper than in the UK.

The UK's active, although sometimes surly, membership of the European Union meant that travel to the continent was relatively cheap and easy. It had suddenly become quite easy for British builders, plumbers, electricians and other trades to set up business in Spain.

Others, who may have had no previous experience of the job, decided to set up shop as estate agents, tour representatives and shopkeepers in Spain. It was a heady time, and there was a strong positive feeling that the doors of a previously closed, often repressive and grey UK had suddenly opened to reveal a glimpse of a sunny and happier world.

Many British people, such as ourselves, were tempted. As well as a wide choice of properties, Spanish mortgages were easy to come by. Banks and finance companies were ready and waiting to offer any help that they could, but at a price.

Once we had chosen and agreed to purchase our new home in the Costa Blanca - a beautiful but small villa on the edge of a new development in a rapidly growing part of the Costa Blanca, we were introduced to a Spanish bank.

I don't actually remember applying to open an account, but presumably we did, since we were suddenly presented with the account details and debit cards. It was of course essential to have a Spanish bank account to live in Spain, and initially we were grateful that this had been done for us. It was after gathering more information about the bank and visiting their local branch, that we felt uneasy.

It was clearly a bank that operated mainly in South America and, by all accounts, had strong links with the drug cartels. Indeed, it appeared that money laundering was one of their many achievements. We closed our account, amidst some difficulty and implied threats that we had to maintain the account with the bank.

After some research, we opened an account with a bank that was jointly owned by both German and Spanish companies. It appeared very settled and staid and we could find no negative reports in the Internet. Indeed, it was recommended by a friendly coach driver, who we had got to know and trusted, as well as several of our friends. It was a bank that we stayed with during our entire time in Spain and the Canary Islands, and recommended to others.

Over time, and for various purposes, we had reason to open an account with another bank, this time in our Canarian village. This was a delight, since the small branch had a cash dispenser outside that made a visit into our nearest town unnecessary. There were two banks in our village, but shortly after the peak of the financial crisis, both bank branches closed. I remember receiving a letter telling us that "for our convenience, our account had been moved to another nearby branch" which was five miles away; convenience indeed!

We felt sorry for the village community, many of whom were unemployed and relied on benefits. Many had no alternative, but to use an inconvenient and irregular bus service, since they had no car. A few months later, although the cash dispenser outside one of the banks remained, it ceased working.

Banking in Spain was always a bit of a nightmare. Lengthy queues were inevitable and there seemed to be a general attitude that banks were there purely for their convenience and that of their staff; customers rarely entered the equation, and were usually regarded as irrelevant.

There always seemed to be a delight in "the computer says no" in responses to even the simplest of requests. Even the simplest of transactions entered on a computer screen always involved sheets of printed paper that had to be 'bonked' with an official stamp. Over time, this time-consuming process became a bit of a joke, and was nearly always entertaining, despite having to waste a morning achieving very little.

Over time, we met some helpful banking staff who seemed to regard David and I as something of an English novelty, and used to delight in practicing their English on us. This was a little annoying, since we wanted these opportunities to practice our Spanish, but this was rarely possible. On these occasions, we sped through queues with alarming speed, which seemed to prove that the bank could be efficient if it chose to be so.

One of our worst experiences has been closing our Spanish bank accounts and credit cards. There appears to be an alarming reluctance for banks to allow this. Due to circumstances beyond our immediate control, David and I left the Canary Islands before we had the opportunity to close several of our accounts.

At the time of leaving the island, which was in haste due to Brexit deadlines for our dogs and cat, I assumed that one of us would return to sell our property and to close any outstanding financial business. This proved to be difficult, since it was to be nearly three years before our house was sold in the Canary Islands. It was also impossible for us to return to the island since we had entered a period of lockdown. In addition, my health diagnosis prevented overseas travel. We have recently completed a period of closing various bank and card accounts by telephone. It most cases, it has been difficult, but not impossible.

Fortunately, the sale of our property has been completed with the help of our excellent lawyer for whom we had fortunately given power of attorney, but sadly this did not include closing bank accounts. One bank simply refused, and continues to refuse to close the account unless we attend a branch in Spain in person. During our current circumstances, this is impossible, so we will leave this account in limbo, no doubt continuing to attract hefty charges that will never be repaid. Sadly, this experience is not unusual, as I recall an elderly friend, who had to travel to Spain briefly to undertake a similar task with another bank, despite having serious health problems.

Moving back to the UK, and getting used to British banking once again, has been a refreshing delight. Despite my distrust of all banks, I have been pleasantly surprised by my contacts with, for example, the Nationwide, who have been surprisingly helpful, and challenger banks, such as Starling and Monzo. These challenger banks show a refreshing new attitude, and although Spain had the beginnings of a similar online bank, I was insufficiently brave to experiment with it.

It has not all been easy though, since my initial requests for a UK credit card, for example, were rejected because I had not lived in the UK for at least three years, not on the electoral roll etc. There are always ways around such issues, and I was quickly able to overcome their refusal.

Another disappointment was that a UK bank that we would like to have banked with, the Co-operative Bank, had financial troubles of its own and was no longer a mutual espousing the issues that we believe in. We have been disappointed to see that many bank branches in the UK have now closed; some of their impressive premises are now hosting firms of solicitors or, more likely, have been turned into yet another coffee or betting shop.

In Teignmouth, for example, I recall at least three banks operating in the town a few years ago; this has now been reduced to one, and even its future is uncertain. Surprisingly, I occasionally see other banks represented in the town by mobile banking vans, but I am not sure that this supports the needs of a mostly elderly population in a way that they would like.

I hope that the Post Office remains open and continues to offer banking services. No doubt that too will in time close, and be absorbed into yet another branch of WH Smith.

World Beating or What?

We are often told by Johnson and his right-wing colleagues that, on any number of issues, "the UK is world beating". Of course, anyone with common sense, and with the ability to do some basic research on the Internet, quickly discovers that this is not true.

We are often told by Johnson and his right-wing colleagues that, on any number of issues, "the UK is world beating". Of course, anyone with common sense, and with the ability to do some basic research on the Internet, quickly discovers that this is not true and is indeed yet another lie designed to calm the post Brexit malaise.

One dangerous example, often quoted, is that the NHS is "world beating". It is not, since data clearly shows that most countries within the EU report much higher survival rates for cancer, cardiovascular and a range of other serious issues, with the UK often trailing near the bottom of the league tables.

One area where the UK is "world beating' is that the UK successfully relies upon and exploits its health workers with low pay and unreasonable working conditions, with the result that health outcomes are high in relation to the money it spends on the health service. Is that "world beating"? I think not.

It is also claimed that the UK's newly adopted policy of shipping vulnerable refugees, who Government claim have entered the UK by a variety of dubious means, to Ruanda for "processing".

Apparently, this ill thought out, dangerous approach to vulnerable refugees seeking help is "world beating", possibly because very few other countries, other than Australia, refuse to do the same. Is this "world beating"? I don't think so.

Where the Government has a right to claim the meaningless title of "world beating" is the growing number of foodbanks that are now a common sight in the UK over the last fifteen years or so. Yes, that is certainly a growth industry and can be fairly claimed as "world beating". Another success story for the UK?

The UK is "world beating" in pomp and circumstance too. No-one does a good state funeral, together with all the military trimmings, better than the Brits. Apparently, it was a tight run thing many years ago, when Germany claimed the title, but that was quickly rectified and the UK can now very fairly claim to be "world beating" when it comes to state funerals, and military processions, as will be discussed later in this chapter.

At the time of writing this chapter, the sad news that Queen Elizabeth had died has been announced. We are currently in the grip of state mourning as we head towards the state funeral. Television, newspapers and other media are completely wrapped up in endless mind-numbing events leading to the funeral, and woe betide any republican daring to express their reservations at such a time for the nation.

I confess to having very mixed emotions about the passing of the Queen. I support the long overdue reform of the House of Lords, with abolition being my preferred option; I would like to see the ending of 'Empire' medals, such as the OBE, MBE etc with their horrific links to Empire days.

I would also like to see state recognition being given to 'real' people who have done something truly positive and worthwhile for society, rather than the usual rush of floosies, temporary sporting stars and over rated celebrities. I look forward to a time when the monarch is no longer head of the 'state church', the Church of England, which is complete nonsense, as is having a 'state church' anyway. As for the monarchy itself, well that is quite another issue.

Despite my strong views on many of these issues, I retain a deep admiration and respect for a mother, grandmother and for someone who had a deep sense of duty over 70 years, which she promised to the nation at the beginning of her reign.

Would it be in the country's best interests to abolish the monarchy in favour of a Presidential system? Would we really gain from having a President, such as Trump, Putin, Bolsonaro in post? Maybe in the UK we would get a President Blair or President Johnson instead; the very thought sickens me. Maybe we should stick to the House of Windsor, at least we know what we will be getting for the next few generations.

Much of the pomp and circumstance that I am currently seeing this week includes overhead shots of Balmoral, Edinburgh, Buckingham Palace and other significant buildings. I see soldiers dressed in all their finery, strutting around with a chest full of medals. Some of the overhead scenes remind me simply of Lego characters, frozen in time; merely a delightful, but meaningless parody of 'Toytown Britain'.

The sight of a much loved, but dead Queen being carried or flown over Scotland and England distresses me. Moving her frail, lifeless body on a gun carriage, simply to lie in state for several days seems, to me, disrespectful rather than respectful, and, in some ways is a cruel end to a life well lived. This is someone's mother and grandmother, and not just a lifeless corpse to be paraded anywhere and everywhere merely to satisfy morbid public curiosity and grief.

My mind wanders briefly to death in the Canary Islands where, after death, the speed of burial or cremation of the body is of the essence and rarely lasts for longer than three days. Obviously, this is for practical reasons, since bodies 'go off' rather quickly in the heat. Surely, mourning the Queen and all the other accompanying paraphernalia didn't have to take so long?

Over the years, the UK has followed the highs and lows of this often-mystical family, and it is often treated as a soap opera. Revelations about the relationship between Charles and Camilla, the death of Princess Diana, as well as sex scandals involving Prince Andrew, to name just a few 'indiscretions', are just a small number of incidents that have rocked the Royal family. However, this is not unique to the UK, since the Spanish monarchy also had many troubles of its own.

Spain's previous King, Juan Carlos, came to the Spanish throne in 1975, following the death of his mentor, the dictator Franco. He managed to achieve a stable democracy, and his reputation was confirmed when he managed to thwart an attempted coup. His popularity remained for several years until the financial crisis brought a number of serious issues to a head that were greatly damaging to the King and monarchy. The King abdicated two years later and moved to Abu Dhabi to avoid further embarrassment to the new King Felipe V1.

The new King is working hard to make the royal family more transparent and agreeable to the Spanish public. Despite this, overall popularity for the Spanish King and the Spanish royal family is low, but they do have the benefit of a media that remains discreet and generally respectful that will help to sustain it until better times come along.

In the UK, the monarchy is safe this week and maybe for a few months ahead, but questions will soon be asked once again whether or not the monarchy, in its present form, is relevant to modern times. In the right-wing tabloids, current respectful and sometimes fawning articles and photos about a much-loved Queen will soon revert to their usual poisonous attacks upon individual members of the royal family.

Rituals such as we have seen over the last ten days or so were designed specifically to encourage the public to form an attachment to the monarchy, as well as being a political reminder of 'Britain's glorious past'. Many do not realise that despite being told that such rituals, parades and ceremonies have evolved from centuries of royal tradition, in reality many of the 'traditions' are newly invented or reinvented. One prime example being the moving 'Vigil of the Princes' when the Queen's children 'stood guard' around the Queen's coffin for 15 minutes.

The clamour from republicans, as well as other countries such as Australia and a number of Caribbean island states, claiming independence from the British monarchy will surely increase, spreading yet more doubt and uncertainty across a country that is already ill at ease with itself and its new place in the world following loss of Empire and the Brexit fallout.

Maybe one answer to the conundrum that the UK is clearly about to face is how to reshape and restore the monarchy in a form that is fit for modern times? Maybe the answer is in Scandinavia?

Following the passing of Queen Elizabeth, Queen Margrethe II of Denmark is now Europe's longest serving monarch. She is 82 years old, a widow, an artist, chain smoker, and an immensely popular monarch, Margrethe was crowned in 1972, but notably at the time of her accession, only 45 per cent of Danes were in favour of maintaining the monarchy.

Today, the monarchy enjoys the support of over 80 per cent of the population. Margrethe is credited with modernising the institution and making it relevant to present day circumstances. She has encouraged the marriage of her two sons to non-nobility and is praised for remaining non-political and scandal-free.
Over the next few days, Kings, Queens, Presidents and Prime Ministers, including the American President, will be heading to Westminster Abbey for the funeral of Queen Elizabeth.

I suspect this will be largest gathering of world leaders that the UK has ever seen or likely to see again. Military pomp will be at its height, and I am sure that the UK will pull off a magnificent, pompous, unforgettable staged event. I have no doubt that on this occasion, the UK will be "world beating'.

A Spiritual Journey

The 'live and let live' attitudes of people in this wonderful island have always been an inspiration to us, and so much in contrast to the narrow, judgemental and often cruel experiences and attitudes that we had experienced in the UK, some of which very sadly continue today.

This is where I move quietly into the spiritual journey part of this book. I wrote this and the following chapters at a time of shock and general confusion about the path in life that has suddenly opened for me.

I was initially uncertain whether to include these chapters or not, so I hope readers will forgive me if the next chapters seem a little self-indulgent. I felt I had to include them so that readers would be able to share and understand our life in Spain and the Canary Islands, as well as our return to the UK. In many ways, it also concludes my first book 'Letters from the Atlantic'.

We celebrated our 50 years anniversary in April. It was over 50 years ago that I met my partner, lover and best friend, David, when we were both studying at teacher training college.

Looking back over the years, I recall difficult times for gay men and women and conclude that we did well to get through it and still be together in a loving relationship that remains as strong today as it did over fifty years ago.

Fifty years ago, relationships between same sex couples were illegal, we were unable to share our feelings with anyone, knowing full well that any hint of our relationship would mean expulsion from teacher training and making a future in our chosen careers impossible.

Over the years, we learned successfully how to hide our feelings, to be vague and non-committal about 'girlfriends'. We 'hid' quietly in a Dorset village, only maintaining a very tight circle of close, reliable friends and never discussing the issue with our families.

Looking back, it was a lonely and, in some ways, an unfulfilling period of our lives. David's skills as an organist became quickly known to local vicars and church leaders, who were desperate for both increased congregations, as well as a reliable and talented organist. Despite this, as soon as there was any hint that we might be a couple, the shutters came down, and invitations to church and community events quickly disappeared.

Against this backdrop, and perhaps surprisingly, I was appointed as the deputy headteacher of a Catholic school. Apparently, I was appointed to keep the visiting nuns and headteacher from quarrelling, as well as impressing the school governors with my skills in debating long-held beliefs in vegetarianism and animal welfare.

Later, both David and I became headteachers of Church of England schools. Once again, secrecy was essential and I recall the school governors looking horrified when I was asked after my interview if I would care to move into the dilapidated school house with my wife. "Maybe she could help with the choir," began the Lady of the Manor. The governors appeared shocked when I politely declined. I am sure that the Governors wished they had asked 'that question' before appointing me as their new headteacher.

Our busy lives as headteachers provided a period of relative stability, mainly because David and I knew how to play the 'I am not gay' game rather well. We could never attend each other's school functions, or attend staff 'get togethers' and or talk about our weekends, as is usual with most school staff.

As usual, we had to remain aloof and non-committal. Even our families believed that we were just "good friends", although this view was dismissed many years later by my young nephew who claimed that they knew all along. How we wish they had told us; it would have made life so much easier!

One memorable day, David had a breakdown. He was very ill and was told that he would never work again. Much was due to work-related stress as a headteacher, as well as what the psychologist described as "repressed sexuality".

David was put on permanent medication and retired from teaching. It has always been a great sadness for me that an excellent teacher and headteacher ended an otherwise successful career in this way.

I continued my working life as a school inspector for OFSTED in England and Estyn in Wales. I enjoyed the job, not only for the privilege of working with so many talented people, who were committed to doing their best for the children in their care, but the escape that it gave me.

I was in a different school every fortnight, leading a different team of inspectors. These were people that I had a professional relationship with, but we rarely had time to talk about our personal lives, and we would probably never meet again; it was the kind of non-committal relationship that suited me just fine.

Working away from home meant that David spent a lot of time on his own, which was not a healthy situation for either of us. We decided to move to Bournemouth, which was one of the best steps that we could have made at that time.

My relationship with God has been severely tested over the years. I had explored a number of spiritual journeys, visiting Baptist, Methodist, Anglican, Catholic, United Reformed and other churches. All made me feel that, as a gay man I was not welcome. I was excluded, always on the outside looking in.

The best way that I can describe it was searching for 'the Light', which was clearly not switched on for gay men and women, and certainly not for me. Neither did I feel comfortable in the traditional 'White Jesus' worship, when I had read and began to explore Buddhism, Hinduism and other faiths. Why did I have to choose a particular brand when I had already suspected that we were all sharing similar faith experiences?

One day we found ourselves joining a service at the Metropolitan Community Church in Bournemouth. It was a revelation and a treasured memory that I will never forget. David and I entered the building and spotted a huge illuminated purple cross glowing from the front of the church.

The pastor at that time ran down the aisle to greet us, and beaming with arms outstretched. "Welcome boys", he said warmly, grasping our hands. It was the first genuine welcome that we had ever received in a church; it was wonderful to experience, which I will never forget.

Metropolitan Community Church in Bournemouth was at that time best described as "a church for broken people". Gay, lesbian, transgendered, the confused, straight, alcoholics, the homeless and the drug dependent were all welcome.

It was a wonderful mix of humanity; we learned so much and made many good friends, and many of whom we are still in contact with today. We both felt that we were meant to be there and savoured every moment of our new relationship with the Spirit and our new-found friends. This church was also incredibly supportive of David's condition, and much of his growing recovery was due to the warmth, support and blessing of this amazing community.

Over time we both began to feel uncomfortable with some of the theology and the 'happy, clappy' side to worship. I was also uneasy about taking a white European Christian approach to my relationship with God, or 'the Light' as we began to call it.

As much as we admired the gifted and inspirational pastor and his team, I had a strong feeling of "Why do I need a middleman in my relationship with God?" Maybe I don't, but I freely accept that there are many who do, and find this relationship both comforting and reassuring.

Who are we to judge? I started being aware of the life and teachings of George Fox and other Quakers. Our pastor was about leave Bournemouth to take on a new challenge in the US, and for us it was also time to take the next step in our spiritual journey. Bournemouth Quakers, here we come!

When we entered the Meeting House for the first time, we were warmly greeted by one of the wardens who took time to explain what would happen at the Meeting. We met many other wonderful, warm-hearted people who took us under their wings.

We felt immediately at home and became members in 2000. It was a time when I began to feel the warmth and spiritual support in personal worship that had been sorely missing in my other church experiences. Wisdom shared during Meetings opened new challenges and areas to explore. Of course, these Meetings were always followed by often noisy discussions, as well as laughter over a welcome coffee.

In 2003, we felt that another significant change in our lives was needed. We had often talked about moving to Spain, which was already a favourite holiday destination.

I continued to be concerned about David's health, and continued medication. As for me, I was becoming increasingly disenchanted with the OFSTED school inspection process, which had moved from one of supportive discussion with school staff about the best way to move a school forward, to an adversarial system that seemed intent upon breaking down goodwill and making matters worse. I decided to quit my work as a school inspector, and in discussion with David planned our move to Spain.

One of the reasons that David and I get on so well is that once we make up our minds, we simply get on with it. Within a few weeks we had moved to our new home in the Costa Blanca.

What a breath of fresh air that was. Our next-door neighbours were a gay couple; we had a lesbian couple living opposite, and a few doors down was a middle-aged couple, who had a gay son and didn't quite know how to cope with it. Indeed, our new home was in a street named San Gabriel, which we were told is the patron saint of gay people, but this might be an exaggeration. Within a couple of weeks, David was pain free and no longer needed any medication. Within a couple of months, David had been interviewed and appointed as the manager of the office of an English-speaking publication, intended for the British community.

I resumed my working life delivering newspapers, and later became a reporter and photographer for the same newspaper. The paper was owned and managed by a gay man, and all the staff, apart from one confused secretary, were all gay.

Upon the advice of our Spanish lawyer, we became the first couple in that region of Spain to enter into a civil partnership, which was a truly memorable event. A wonderful time of healing had begun and we no longer felt like outsiders looking in.

A couple of years later, our boss declared that he wanted to expand the newspaper as it was doing so well. I suggested the Canary Islands, and our boss asked us to prepare a business plan for him to consider.

Not ones to waste time, three weeks later, David and I were on a ferry to the Canary Islands accompanied by our two dogs, Barney and Bella, and a laptop computer. We were to launch and manage a new English language newspaper in Gran Canaria, and with an intention to launch across the seven islands.

Amazingly, Gran Canaria was one place where we had always wanted live, but thought impossible. There we were, with a full-time contract and covered by the Spanish Health Service. We were indeed fortunate.

The 'live and let live' attitudes of people in this wonderful island have always been an inspiration to us, and so much in contrast to the narrow, judgemental and often cruel experiences and attitudes that we had experienced in the UK, some of which very sadly continue today.

Our work editing the newspaper was often challenging, but we were always refreshed and invigorated by wonderful people from so many nationalities that we worked and enjoyed being with. I also began my work as a published author, writing crime thrillers, as well as books about living and working in Spain and the Canary Islands.

Our thoughts and prayers often returned to Bournemouth Meeting. We would usually sit together with Barney and Bella and a lighted candle at 10.30 am on Sunday mornings, in an attempt to link with Bournemouth Friends.

One day we had a knock at the door. It was a Belgian couple, long-term Quakers, who had attended a Meeting in Stuttgart and seen our names in a Quaker magazine living in Gran Canaria. They visited the island often, and wondered if we could meet together on Sundays? It was such a strange coincidence, or was it? As a result, we continued to meet regularly with the Belgian couple in our home for several years until we returned to the UK.

We were joined by a Spanish and German couple, a brilliant Welsh harpist from the island orchestra and a Russian academic who had managed to escape persecution with his partner. The stories that were shared over coffee after our meetings were true eye openers.

During those years, we regarded our house group as a kind of Bournemouth 'outpost', and we continued to receive newsletters and newsy emails from Bournemouth Meeting that inspired us and were readily shared between all members of our house group. Although I doubt that Bournemouth Quakers were ever aware of their Canary Islands link, our Belgian, Spanish, German and Russian friends were certainly well aware of Bournemouth Meeting, and may well visit Bournemouth Meeting one day.

All good things come to an end eventually and, for us, Brexit was the final curtain. We had heard enough of promises from both the UK and Spanish governments to make us uneasy.

We had to make a decision, which would mean the end of our amazing life in the Canary Islands, leaving friends and work that we loved, as well as our lovely home. Nothing is forever and we looked to the future with confidence, as well as some apprehension.

The Elephant in the Room

Death is certainly 'the elephant in the room' for many people. Relatives, visitors and friends of those with a terminal condition often avoid talking about such issues for fear of upsetting the patient.

I have never really understood why Western culture avoids talking about death. As the old adage goes 'Death and taxation are the realities of life.'

Over the years I have concluded that taxation is not one of the ultimate realities after all. Russian oligarchs, Tory 'grandees' and, no doubt, others somehow manage to escape this 'reality', so we are therefore left with only death as the ultimate reality, arbiter and leveller for all. Let's just see it here as 'social levelling and a final liberation' rather than going too much into the theology of it all.

As a Quaker, I try to keep an open mind about such things, and require evidence before I come to a firm conclusion, which is impossible in this case. Death is certainly 'the elephant in the room' for many people. As much as I dislike this phrase, relatives, visitors and friends of those with a terminal condition often avoid talking about such issues for fear of upsetting the patient.

In reality, of course, the opposite is true; it can be deeply upsetting when friends and those that you love avoid talking about something that may be deeply troubling. The bottom line is that it is good to talk and to share feelings, however painful they may be.

We had a very good friend and neighbour in the Canary Islands. Colin was a man with a great sense of humour and generosity, with a clear sense of duty and a strong conviction of how he should behave towards others, and they towards him.

We shared many meals, drinks and much laughter over several years, but it was one day that contact with him all but ceased. Colin was still polite when we met him, but his demeanour was such that we thought that we had done something to upset him.

Maybe Bella was barking too loudly, or maybe he didn't approve of David playing the piano? It was only after several months that I managed to catch him and pin him down to the real reason for his sudden change of behaviour.

Reluctantly, Colin asked us to sit at the patio table where we had shared so many meals, whilst he poured us generous glasses of his favourite red wine. He told us that he had Stage 4 pancreatic cancer and the prognosis was very poor. "We'll still all be able to go out for pizzas, boys," he added cheerfully, but we both knew that was not to be.

Over the next few weeks, Colin became increasingly worse and less mobile. He put on considerable weight, since he was doing little exercise, and palliative care was minimal.

The doctor at our local surgery was very kind and allowed Colin to call in for a lengthy chat whenever he felt like it.

We were not aware of any medical staff, palliative care nurses or social workers ever visiting his home. Ourselves and other neighbours did our best to support him, cooking meals, helping with drugs and lifting him back into his chair whenever he fell, since he was unable to sleep in his bed.

Occasionally we would be awoken with Colin shouting for help as he had fallen on the way to the toilet. By now, he had become so heavy that we could not lift him ourselves, and had to call a neighbour and their two teenage boys to help to lift Colin back into his chair. Despite a social worker being promised to assess Colin's situation, no one ever came.

I contrast this to the levels of support for those at end-of-life stage currently available in the UK. Admittedly, over the last ten to 15 years of Conservative and coalition governments, NHS budgets have been massively reduced and both NHS and social care have reached an all-time crisis, exasperated, of course by COVID, Brexit and other issues.

Despite this, if one shouts loud enough, and coverage is patchy across the country, some help is available to those in most need, generously supported by charities such as Macmillan. The UK is also well supported by a network of hospices throughout the country, which are charitable institutions, but may receive some government funding in some circumstances.

I contrast this to support for similar patients in Spain and the Canary Islands. It is generally accepted in Spanish culture that it is family responsibility to look after those who are elderly, sick or unable to look after themselves.

Many households of Spanish people include several generations, with the youngest looking after those in most need. In hospitals too, it is often family members who help to clean and dress their loved ones, as well as bringing them food. This is not to say that care is not readily available for those who have no family members to care for them, but it does become increasingly difficult for those at end-of-life.

Similarly, the lack of residential care for the elderly, as well as lack of hospices and visiting care staff create considerable problems for those living and working in Spain who are not of Spanish nationality and have no one in the country to look after them.

Whilst living in the Canary Islands, I was aware of several Catholic residential homes, which were mostly intended for the local community. Again, this did not help those in need, such as Colin. Eventually, due to persuasion in the right ears, a good friend of Colin managed to get him admitted into a private hospital, surprisingly paid for by the local government.

This was an unusual arrangement, but recognised the seriousness and helplessness of Colin's condition. For several weeks until his passing, Colin was cared for with dignity, kindness and consideration.

It Ain't Over Until the Fat Lady Sings

The doctor was clear and to the point. I always prefer a no-nonsense approach to serious issues and, at this point, could do without any unnecessary flannel and comforting, yet often meaningless or patronising words.

The nurse led us into a small, brightly lit room. Apart from a number of posters warning about Covid 19 and not to abuse NHS staff, the room was empty, apart from a small, round table and four chairs.

A fresh box of Kleenex tissues had been carefully placed in the middle of the table. David and I glanced at each other and nodded; the box of tissues was a bit of a giveaway. I immediately sensed what was coming.

The doctor, who I had only met briefly at the beginning of the colonoscopy procedure, sat stony faced in one of the chairs. The nurse beckoned to David and I to sit in two of the remaining chairs, whilst she took up a position standing by the door, as if guarding against any possible escape.

I already knew what was to come. As I lay in the recovery room after the examination, I wondered why the nurse asked me for David's phone number. He was sitting in the car outside and I could hear her asking him to come inside for a meeting right away with the doctor. I sensed the urgency in her voice.

The doctor was clear and to the point. I always prefer a no-nonsense approach to serious issues and, at this point, could do without any unnecessary flannel and comforting, yet often meaningless or patronising words.

"It's like this, Barrie," he began. "We have found three polyps during the colonoscopy, but sadly, one of them has turned cancerous. It has developed into quite a large tumour in the bowel, which will have to be removed as soon as possible."

He then went on to draw a sketch of a bowel, which I thought was remarkably good, given the speed of drawing. He looked at me before drawing a line across part of the bowel. "It is this part that will have to come out". He looked at me again.

I nodded, but said nothing.

"We will get this thing out of you as soon as possible. However, I should warn you that there will have to be several scans and these may indicate that cancer has spread elsewhere. At this stage, we do not know, but there is a possibility given the size of the tumour."

At this point, I did have a few questions buzzing around in my head, the main one being "How long have I got?" I decided that to ask that question would be akin to asking "How long is a piece of string?" at this stage, so decided not to ask the question after all.

The doctor then brightened up. "Try not to worry too much about it. We do this type of surgery all the time here. I'll be referring you to one of my colleagues who will discuss this further with you once the biopsy has been examined."

The doctor paused, "Nurse will give you a booklet that will give you more information, and we will contact you very soon with an appointment to see a consultant. Do you have any questions?"

We drove home almost in silence, apart from a few pleasantries about road conditions. Oscar gave us his usual boisterous greeting, and I wandered around the garden with him to get some air. Strangely, I was suddenly aware of how colourful and bright everything had become. Instead, of a grey, dismal garden in the midst of winter, I was now aware of early signs of spring.

Buds were forming on our camellias and magnolias, daffodil shoots were appearing; everywhere I looked, there was life beginning to form once again. For the first time that awful day, I began to feel hopeful of a future after all.

It was a strange coincidence, if you believe in such things, that on the day of the confirmation of my diagnosis, we received a phone call from our estate agent in Gran Canaria. Apparently, they had received a genuine offer for our house at last!

Our house had already been on the market for nearly three years, and apart from a couple of time wasters, there had been very little interest, no doubt due to Covid and Brexit. At last, it looked as if we could finally part with our house and use the proceeds to make our finances more secure. The timing could not have been better.

During the years that we had lived in Gran Canaria, we had sadly lost a number of close friends and acquaintances. Some were the self-inflicted victims of alcohol and drugs, whilst others had passed shortly after their return to the UK.

It was the latter group that always concerned me. I could not understand why several of our friends had passed quite suddenly and unexpectedly shortly after their return to the UK. I assumed that they probably already had undiagnosed health conditions that only became apparent after their return.

Maybe the sudden change in climate, lack of sunlight and other changes had something to do with it. It was a strange phenomenon that I did not understand. I recall thinking that the subject of those returning to the UK dying or becoming very ill upon their return to the UK would make someone a good subject for a PhD thesis one day.

Since my return to the UK in February 1999, I was vaguely aware of a decrease in my energy and general feeling of wellbeing. I had put this down to the stress and hard work of physically making our new home in the UK habitable, as well as all the stress of moving. It was certainly nothing to see a doctor about.

People who know me well, will be aware of my love of gadgets, and particularly of the Apple variety. I have been a fan of the Apple Watch since the first model came onto the market and regularly upgraded to the latest model over the years. I have been fascinated that it could check my heart rate, monitor my exercise, as well as a whole host of wonderful things. One issue that did trouble me was the occasional and later more frequent warning of "Atrial Fibrillation".

This concerned me, but not enough to see a doctor, as I was far too busy trying to move home. Covid 19 also entered the situation, and we were soon in lockdown; it would have seemed foolish to waste a doctor's time simply because my watch had given me a warning.

After nearly 70 warnings on my watch, a general feeling of no energy, together with losing my sense of taste and increasing difficulty in swallowing, I telephoned our surgery one morning, and the GP asked me to go in to see her that afternoon.

She listened carefully to my attempts at self-diagnosis, checked me over, and suggested that I have blood test. The doctor seemed confident that it wasn't atrial fibrillation, but suggested that I have this checked out as there could be other reasons why the heart wasn't behaving normally.

The doctor was correct. I had several tests on the heart, which seemed to be behaving normally, but the blood test revealed that I had severe anaemia.

There was blood loss that had to be investigated. This discovery led to both an endoscopy, as well as a colonoscopy, and a CT scan. I also had two large infusions of iron, which rapidly increased my energy levels. I was so grateful to both my GP and the NHS for giving me such prompt access to tests, despite the huge burdens that Covid was putting on the service.

The thought of dying focuses the mind rather wonderfully. I am not afraid of death, but more afraid about how it might happen. We all wish for a pain-free end to our lives, as it is the big inevitable, along with taxation.

As a Quaker, I have learned to accept that death is part of life and to accept loss. Accepting loss is the difficult part. My main concern is, of course, my partner David. I know that the pain of loss is the price that we pay for love, but it is that part of dying that bothers me most.

I began to think of the will that we both prepared some years ago. We had decided that we would be buried, eventually together, in a woodland cemetery; no headstones or memorials, just the planting of a special tree.

That was before we moved to Spain. When we moved to Spain, we quickly became aware that burials did not mean burying in the ground in a churchyard or cemetery, but instead the body would be popped into a kind of drawer in what looked like very large stone filing cabinets.

There the body would remain for five or ten years, depending upon how long the rental agreement was, before being removed and placed in some kind of communal grave. It made sense of course, because over many years there would never be enough filing cabinets to fit everyone in.

In view of the temporary nature of the intended final resting place, David and I decided that cremation would be the best option after all. I immediately added a codicil to my will to that effect.

The next difficult part was telling our family and friends. Fortunately, everyone was supportive, expressing concern and support but without being overwhelming, which I had feared.

As much as I appreciate the value of Facebook for keeping in contact with family and friends, particularly whilst living overseas, I want to avoid using Facebook as a kind of running commentary about my deteriorating condition, which would presumably be depressing and pointless.

At this stage, I am also far too vain to be photographed without hair. No doubt this will change, so I must be on the lookout for a decent selection of hats!

I posted a brief statement that I would be leaving Facebook for a while. After my surgery, I decided to post a regular photo of one of my collection of flowering orchids, just to let friends and family know that I am still alive and kicking, but to avoid inflicting unnecessary concern and misery upon others, as far as possible. After all, what could be better that seeing a cheerful, bright yellow orchid in the middle of winter?

My diagnosis was followed by what seemed like an endless round of blood tests, consultations and scans. A CT scan was quickly followed by an MRI scan and then a PET CT scan in Plymouth.

It was there that they discovered that the cancer had spread to my liver. Later, my consultant told me that surgery was not going to be possible on the liver, as my liver was a strange shape. However, chemotherapy would hopefully help to slow the aggressive nature of the disease.

The next major event in my cancer experience was removal of the tumour from my bowel. I was booked into hospital for five days; I was given plenty of literature to help me to prepare for the operation, as well as what to do afterwards.

Surgery was lengthy, but it went well, given that it was a keyhole experience, but also some rather larger incisions to remove the cancer. My intended start in hospital of five days, turned out to be nearly two weeks, due to complications.

My bowel would not behave as it should and there was concern that I was getting weaker due to not eating in over two weeks. Doctors threatened to add a feeding tube to my already impressive collection of annoying tubes fixed to various parts of my body.

Nausea was one of my big issues, which was not surprising given that I was surrounded by several patients, including myself, who were unable to control their bowel movements.

The serving of breakfast took place in a ward that smelled of shit and vomit, particularly overnight and first thing in the morning, whilst blood tests were being taken simultaneously. Nursing staff wondered why I felt so nauseous, seemingly unable to understand the reasons why. I won't go into too much detail about the failings in personal care during my stay in that ward, as it will make me seem ungrateful, which I am not.

Nursing staff that were available worked tirelessly and were clearly exhausted. Without the support of student nurses sent from Plymouth University to help out, I really do not know what would have happened. These were difficult and challenging times for all.

There was one very bad night when I fell into the depths of depression and felt that I could no longer cope with what was happening to me. Desperate to get to the toilet, and connected to oxygen, a saline drip and a tube in my stomach I felt unable to get myself to the toilet in the corridor in time.

I pressed the help button and as experienced by other patients in our small ward, it was a good fifteen minutes before anyone appeared to help, by which time it was too late.

This happened on several occasions. It was at this point I made up my mind to ask David to get me out of this hell hole into a private hospital, possibly even getting my nephew to collect me in his builder's van, tubes, drips and all.

In the morning, I realised that my earlier thoughts were nonsense, there was no doubt that it was the drugs that were talking. I simply had to put up with it, and pray that I could soon escape. Fortunately, things did get a little better and I was finally discharged.

With David's love and care, I made a good recovery from the surgery. David ensures that I am fed nutritiously very regularly and, at the time of writing, those that see me tell me how well I look.

I started on the first round of chemotherapy, which went quite well, apart from always feeling tired and some nausea. My oncologist has been very kind, helpful and supportive, but the news hasn't always been very good.

Knowing that I value facts and not flannel, he eventually admitted that I had around two years left to live, as the cancer had spread to the liver. This was later reduced to one year when a later scan revealed that the chemotherapy had no effect on reducing cancer on the liver; indeed, it had grown.

One friend, Bob, who also had cancer, wrote to me before he passed, telling me that it is an 'individual experience', I guess I know now what he meant by these carefully chosen words. I have come to terms with what is happening and hope that the chemotherapy gives me more quality time to enjoy with David and those that I love. I have hope, but no expectations.

All lives are a journey. We often have choices about the paths that we take, but some paths are chosen for us. The paths that we take are an adventure; some we take with others, whilst others we take alone. In all our journeys through life, we hope for something exciting, maybe a new beginning, seeking peace and relaxation or simply something different.

I have found joy in creating and writing my articles and books. In many ways, I see writing as a journey, an adventure in exploring the unknown and unfamiliar. I have also found that, as in my writing, I am often shunted from one safe space to another, without conscious planning or warning. In each case, it has been a wonderful and enriching experience, which I have never regretted.

Life and death are adventures; at this stage I do not know what will happen, or how this will end, but my hope is that this is the beginning of another enriching chapter in my life.

"May you have the hindsight to know where you've been, the foresight to know where you are going, and the insight to know when you have gone too far."
Irish Proverb and Blessing

Printed in Great Britain
by Amazon